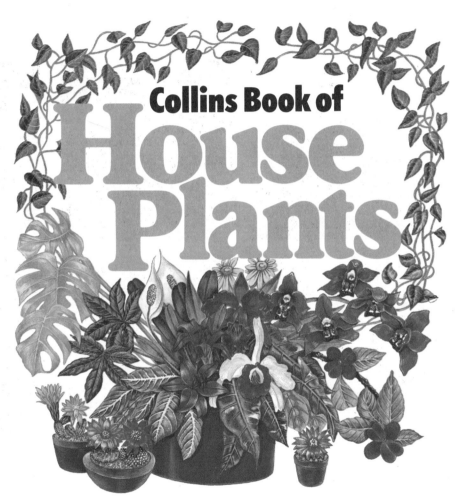

Collins Book of House Plants

Edited by Leslie Johns

Collins Glasgow & London

Translated by Caroline Bidwell

This edition
© 1977 William Collins Sons
and Company Ltd
Originally published.in
Italian as Angolo Verde
© 1974 Fratelli Fabbri
Editori, Milan

Designed by Berkeley Publishers Ltd,
9 Warwick Court, London WC1

Printed in Great Britain
ISBN 0 00 435401 X (cased)
　　　 0 00 435402 8 (paperback)

Contents

Step into the world of houseplants, says Leslie Johns

THE *Collins Book of Houseplants* makes a splendid introduction to a fascinating hobby. The book originated in Italy but in its present form it has been re-styled and edited to make it more serviceable for English readers. Tastes in plants and in decorative room styles differ from country to country and climatic differences must also be taken into account.

But the Italians have a great sense of style and this, I believe, is reflected in the pictures in this book.

Years ago houseplants—apart from the odd aspidistra—were the prerogative of the wealthy. In Victorian times they reached a high point in conservatory culture. Today, few of us can live in such an expansive style. Fortunately, we know a good deal more today about plant culture, and modern methods of propagation have brought even the more exotic plants within reach of the average pocket.

This book has been edited and prepared with this vast new army of houseplant enthusiasts in mind. Each plant has an 'identity card' which gives in an easily understood form all the necessary facts about the plant and also tells you how to care for it.

There is a plant for every place and occasion. And plants, as these pages tell us, have their own special language. 'Say it with flowers' is not just an idle phrase.

We have tried to avoid unnecessary technicalities, although the plants and their families are given their correct botanical names. All these plants are readily available in this country and all of them will thrive in our homes if we tend them with due care.

Houseplants, I believe, enrich a home far beyond their price. They can add grace and a touch of luxury. And, for town dwellers especially, they bring that necessary element of nature into the most boxlike block of flats.

Above all, houseplants are fun. Anyone who has experienced the thrill of watching a trailing plant creep round a bare corner will know what I mean.

They also make delightful gifts and this book will help you to add intelligently selected gifts to your friends' collections if you are feeling generous.

Here then, is the world of houseplants. Enjoy it. For plants, whether indoors or outdoors, provide a special therapy for us all.

INTRODUCTION

Until the early years of this century it was almost unheard of for the ordinary person to keep ornamental tropical plants indoors. That was a privilege reserved for the very rich who could afford a heated conservatory.

In the huge glass rooms of the 18th-century conservatory belonging to the Empress Catherine of Russia, heated as they were by vast underground furnaces, there flourished all kinds of flowering plants, tropical greenery and exotic birds, even in the depths of winter. But in the houses of the less rich, where methods of heating for humans, let alone plants, left much to be desired, only the aspidistra, begonias and a few types of Mediterranean palm had any hope of survival.

Today, of course, things have changed. It is easier to control the lighting, temperature and humidity level indoors, and whether you live in a town flat or a country cottage you can gain great pleasure from cultivating an enormous range of plants for your home.

A great variety of bulbs, foliage and flowering plants, cacti and succulents can easily be obtained at reasonable prices from garden centres and florist shops, and with a little care and knowledge, should last for many years.

The aim of this book is to show you how to look after and enjoy your houseplants, how to keep them in first class condition to prolong their life, and to deal with any problems that might arise. Plants usually die as a result of ignorance rather than neglect, and this can be prevented if you learn about and understand their various idiosyncrasies and requirements. Many plants are now sold with instructions for care, but these are frequently lost and cuttings from friends soon wither if not properly looked after.

The *Book of Houseplants* is divided into three main sections. The first section offers practical advice on the care of plants—watering, nutrition, light, humidity and room temperature, soil, repotting, propagation and any necessary additional care. Common problems encountered are dealt with, and there are suggestions on how you can make the most of your plants to enhance your home.

Section two is the main guide to specific varieties of bulbs and houseplants, and covers flowering plants, green and coloured foliage plants, succulents and cacti. The third section contains a work calendar and gives helpful information on special techniques such as hydroponics, bottle gardens, Bonsai, Ikebana and flower arranging.

SECTION ONE: PLANT CARE

Growing houseplants is not an enormous problem provided a few essential and simple rules are followed. The following pages provide a few fundamental points on how to look after houseplants. (The rules for individual plant care are under the appropriate plant headings.)

On this and some of the following pages, we show a number of interesting ways of arranging indoor plants.
1. This vase adds a touch of elegance to a rather austere setting.
2. This group of dieffenbachia, syngonium and ficus plants helps to soften the harsh line of the column.
3. This arrangement creates a pretty green corner, and at the same time acts as an excellent room divider.
4. Houseplants can successfully be grown in between the double glazing of a window. Plants such as scindapsus, philodendron, croton and ferns are particularly suitable, as are many flowering varieties such as the euphorbia. This system creates a

mini-greenhouse with a constant level of humidity and a reasonably cool temperature, both of which help to create ideal conditions for indoor plants.
5. A dieffenbachia grown in water. This system ensures that the plant will live for a long time and that its foliage will stay in good condition.

5

WATERING

1. Containers with their own in-built water supply greatly simplify the task of watering.
2. This particular method of watering allows the water to trickle slowly through the soil, keeping it moist for many days.

3. Other examples (see opposite page) of an effective plant display in which the plants are all grown in water.

One of the most difficult aspects of growing house-plants is watering, especially if the plants are to maintain their luxuriant appearance indoors. Like human beings and animals, plants require a certain amount of humidity if they are to survive. Water transports the necessary nutrients to the leaves, which manufacture essential materials for plant growth; it fills the cells of the leaves, keeping them turgid and healthy.

The atmosphere in many houses tends to be very dry, especially in winter, when the windows are not opened very much to let in fresh air and moisture. This dryness in the atmosphere, added to the evaporation caused if the owner has central heating, can cause considerable damage.

The most frequent question asked by people buying plants is how often should they be watered? It is not always easy to answer, as so many factors are involved, such as room temperature, humidity, whether it is summer or winter and, obviously, much depends on the type of plant. Knowledge can really only be gained by experience in attempting to gauge the correct balance between a wet, muddy soil, and a soil which is too dry. To find out whether a plant needs watering, you should feel the soil with the fingertips. If the earth feels cool and moist, then it does not need watering yet, but when it feels dry and dusty, if the pot gives a hollow ring when tapped and if the pot-ball can be lifted easily out of the pot, then the plant should be watered immediately.

Make sure that you do not use cold water; the water you use should be at room temperature and the best way of ensuring this is to leave it in the watering-can in the room in which the plants live for several hours before use. If possible, collect rainwater to water the plants. As plants grow more rapidly in summer than in winter, there is more danger of underwatering rather than overwatering but in winter, when temperatures are low, the reverse applies. Because the plant's roots must have room to breathe, it is essential that they never become waterlogged through overwatering. Excessive water in the soil prevents the easy respiration on which absorption depends, causing the plant to droop. This often happens when it has been left standing in a saucer of water. To treat a waterlogged plant you should put the plant in a shady place, let the soil become almost dry, then water in very small doses so that the soil is just moist, until new roots form.

Some plants, such as succulents, generally require much less water than other house-plants—usually only every 10–14 days—whereas ferns require a great deal. If a succulent plant is being grown in a very hot atmosphere (20–34°C or 70–75°F), it will obviously need more water. The same reasoning applies to ferns: if they are being grown in an unusually cool atmosphere (12–15°C or 55–60°F), they will require less water to keep the soil moist.

In conclusion

Plants should be watered either according to the general instructions given when they are purchased, or according to guidelines laid down by gardening books, but the frequency and amount of water will also depend on the environment in which each particular plant is grown. This will be learned by experience.

Generally speaking, when the uppermost part of the trunk or branches is growing well and new shoots are forming, then the plant is doing well and is being watered correctly. However, if the leaves are drooping or if their surface is opaque and they feel papery to the touch (apart from a few special kinds of 'dry' plant), then the plant is not getting enough water.

It is advisable to spray the leaves of indoor plants frequently in hot and sunny weather (using a special spray with tepid water)—even every day for some types of plant. On the other hand, there are plants which should never be sprayed at all as this could irrevocably damage their leaves (plants with hairy or velvety leaves like the African violet, gloxinia, etc.).

Overwatering and underwatering frequently present the same symptoms—drooping or yellowing foliage; but overwatering is the most prevalent fault in the case of houseplants. It is also most difficult to cure. Water can always be added when it appears necessary, but it cannot be taken away.

The best kind of watering-can for use with houseplants is a small can with a long, thin spout which can easily reach all the plants at the centre of the plant pot or jardinière.

One way of solving all your watering problems is to resort to growing all your plants in water (hydroponics). By this method, the plant roots live constantly immersed in water and can absorb moisture as and when they need it. There are special green glass vases on the market for this purpose, some of which are most attractive.

Watering during the holidays

If you are going away in the summer and cannot arrange for a friend or neighbour to water your plants when you are away, and if you don't have a self-watering device,

3

the best thing to do is place all the plants in the centre of a room that does not get too much sun, trim off any flower buds and water the plants thoroughly. Pack damp peat round the pots and cover the

soil with wet newspaper to keep it moist. If you have a garden, the plants can be dug into the soil in their pots in the shade, where they can absorb all the moisture they need.

When you are away during the winter, the plants will not require so much water. Again, group the plants in the centre of a room away from draughts, water the soil, and pack moist peat round the pots.

FEEDING and NUTRITION

Although standardized composts already contain the correct amount of fertilizer, this will not be sufficient to keep the plant in good condition indefinitely without the addition of other substances.

Generally speaking, this initial dose will keep the plant happy for about three to four months, but after that it is advisable to feed the plant regularly—about once a month in winter and twice in spring and summer—with a well balanced 'diet'. Every vegetable organism needs to absorb a reasonable amount of chemical and organic substances as well as water if it is to form new shoots and flowers.

To ensure this is carried out correctly, the following

points should be remembered:

Any kind of fertilizer, organic or chemical, should be spread on the soil after watering. This will prevent the roots coming into sudden contact with the fertilizer, which could cause considerable damage. If the soil is very dry, the plant might drink up the water too thirstily, absorbing all the fertilizer in one go. This could result in the capillary roots or, even worse, the absorbent hairs on the roots, being badly scorched.

The frequency with which houseplants need feeding obviously varies from species to species. Young plants need

A foliar feed can be given by spraying a hormone stimulant mixture onto the leaves. Make sure furnishings will not suffer.

less feeding than older, more developed ones. Usually a slow-acting organic fertilizer such as bonemeal is used. This is absorbed gradually and should only be administered when planting (or repotting) and in the autumn and spring. A balanced fertilizer should also be used once a month or even more frequently for some plants. A water soluble type, which can be given when watering, is the simplest.

Plants are not wholly dependent on the amount of food given to their roots; they absorb carbon dioxide through the leaf pores and synthesize it to form the starches and sugars necessary for growth. This process is known as photosynthesis. Foliar feeds provide nutritive elements and are necessary in addition to organic and

Houseplants and garden plants both need periodic doses of compound fertilizers; the soluble type is easy to administer when watering.

mineral fertilizers for healthy plants as they help to encourage the formation of new vegetation and generally invigorate the plant. A few drops of hormone stimulant should be mixed with water and then sprayed on the leaves at regular intervals. This will greatly encourage the growth of new leaves and flowers and will increase the flow of sap through the plant tissues.

It is essential that the manufacturer's instructions on the pack should be followed closely as an excess of nutrients can kill plants. Although it might be tempting to feed sick plants, they must *only* be fed when growing healthily—feeding sick, overwatered plants or even young, newly potted ones will burn them up. Weak plants should always be nursed back to health before any food is given. Only feed when the soil is moist, and remember that it is better to feed too little rather than too much.

ADDITIONAL CARE

Three further routines that can be carried out in addition to feeding are spraying, cleaning and polishing.

Spraying
This is a helpful addition to the regular watering routine if houseplants are to be kept healthy. Spraying should be done with a special plastic or brass spray. There are various types at differing prices on the market and they are all simple to use and hardwearing. Spray valves or atomizers which can be fitted to the top

of an ordinary bottle are excellent for those who have only a few houseplants.

If limited time is available, plants can be sprayed as infrequently as once a week, but ideally they should be sprayed daily to keep their leaves shining and healthy. Plants that are sprayed every day will not suffer from the dangerous film of dust that can block the pores on the surface of the leaves and consequently cause problems.

Both leaf polishes and hormone growth stimulants or

foliar feeds can be administered by spraying. Leaf polishes have the dual purpose of coating the leaf with an attractive shiny protective patina while at the same time providing a disinfectant action against various infections.

Keep your houseplants healthy by spraying them with a disinfectant polish every month or so.

Cleaning
Plants with large leaves tend to collect dust and this can be removed by sponging them

gently with plain water.

Polishing
It is also possible to use a special leaf polish to remove the dust and smog particles which often obstruct the 'pores'. If this is not done, the plant could eventually die. As well as helping to clean the leaves, this polish covers them with a shiny protective patina. Many leaf polishes contain a special insecticide and fungicide which will help to protect the plant from the most common pests and diseases.

LIGHT

Light is necessary for all plants to survive and, if deprived of light, they become pale and thin. Many houseplants can live quite happily in positions where there is very little natural light, providing they can be given periods in good light, such as that found in a greenhouse.

In any case, many of our most popular houseplants originated from the jungle where there is often very little light. Even though the actual plants we have in our homes come from local nurseries, rather than straight from Brazil or Java, they still manage to retain the ability to adapt to

life in places which seldom have direct sunlight.

Plants which have been grown in shade must only gradually be introduced to intense sunlight, otherwise the soft tissues will burn. Plants should never be placed on south-facing window-sills when the sun is very strong.

Specific requirements for individual plants are dealt with in the next section but, in general, plants with coloured and variegated leaves require more sunlight to preserve their colour than green foliage houseplants. This is an important point to bear in mind.

HUMIDITY AND ROOM TEMPERATURE

To achieve success in growing healthy houseplants you should try to provide ideal indoor conditions. Many plants are tropical or subtropical in origin and require more warmth and humidity than others. Lack of humidity causes evaporation of water through the plant's leaves. Generally speaking, the higher the room temperature, the greater the level of humidity should be, and in many cases plants are actually better off in a coolish room that has a high humidity level than a hot, dry, centrally-heated room. To increase humidity you should spray your plants regularly with an atomizer spray or, alternatively, place pebbles in the saucers on which your plant pots stand, and pour water into the saucers, making sure that the pebbles are not covered. When the water evaporates it will create a humid atmosphere for your plants.

Extreme changes of temperature are very dangerous to houseplants. Subjection to undue cold may cause chlorosis (yellowing leaves) and is the result of the plant being unable to absorb the necessary nutrients through very cold soil. The room temperature should never drop below 10°C (50°F) for most plants; more delicate varieties should never be exposed to less than 15°C (60°F).

Excessive heat does not damage some houseplants so long as they are not subjected to direct and concentrated heat, continual cold draughts or prolonged sauna baths. There is nothing worse than trying to cool down dehydrated, thirsty plants by opening the window (probably with an outside temperature below freezing point), or by immersing the whole flower pot in a bath of cold water to give it a good cleaning or soaking. Underfloor heating can be very damaging, so if you have this type of heating keep all plant pots and holders above floor level.

SOIL

Obviously an important part of plant growing is selecting the right kind of soil. Fortunately, as far as this requirement is concerned, houseplants fall into three well defined categories:

☐ Plants which require normal moisture (philodendron, dracaena, scindapsus, syngonium, palms, aralia, etc.).

☐ Plants which prefer a great deal of moisture (ferns, African violet, selaginella, pteris, spathiphyllum, etc.).

☐ Plants which like a fairly dry soil and infrequent watering (succulents, sansevieria, ficus, pandanus, billbergia).

Certain ingredients must be added to the soil in varying quantities to control the degree of moisture conductivity (i.e. ability to retain moisture):

Peat
If you want a soil which will retain a normal amount of moisture, add about one-third peat.

Moss
Use bog or sphagnum moss. If a very absorbent soil is required, add about one-third moss.

Sand
When a very permeable soil which will allow the water to drain through very quickly is needed, add about one-quarter to one-third sand.

This should be well washed river sand and not too fine.

Special houseplant composts
What is the best kind of soil to use for houseplants? There are special ready-mixed composts available at flower shops and garden centres. These are suitable for most types of houseplant.

The John Innes (or JI) composts were devised by scientists at the John Innes Horticultural Institution about half a century ago in an attempt to find a single for-

A flower pot covered with sphagnum moss. This moss retains moisture.

mulation for a potting soil to take the place of the many different recipes in use at the time. The JI composts have been standardized and accepted in many parts of the world. They consist of a basic formulation to which fertilizers have been added at varying strengths; thus JI No. 1 is the weakest and suitable for small and delicate plants and JI No. 3 is the strongest and capable of benefiting larger types of trees and shrubs.

There are JI potting composts and JI seed composts. They are normally available virtually everywhere in small quantities but two drawbacks have arisen. In the first place, all suppliers have not always been very meticulous in the way in which they follow the set recipe. They have not screened their basic materials so that roots and stones sometimes appear, or they have not sterilized their basic soils, with the result that weed seeds are not killed. Secondly, as sources of the virgin loam specified are now scarce, less desirable soils have been incorporated. So, although JI mixtures are still useful and widely employed, they are not now as foolproof as they were designed to be.

Because of these facts, horticultural scientists have been searching for other soils or potting composts and in several parts of the world the so-called soil-less composts are most favoured. These are mainly based on peat and they have many advantages. They are light in weight, clean to handle, capable of holding many times their own weight of water yet they also drain well and fertilizers are easily added and mixed. The soil-less composts appear under several proprietory names and because the capital cost of machinery and equipment to produce them is high, their suppliers are always large corporations or specialist producers with good reputations.

In spite of the John Innes composts and the comparatively new soil-less composts, some houseplant enthusiasts and some commercial houseplant growers still believe in special soil mixtures for special plants and prefer to mix their own. One or more of the larger houseplant producers also markets a special houseplant soil under its own brand name.

Re-potting

Here are a few helpful suggestions:

Always put a drainage layer at the bottom of the pot to help prevent the roots from rotting. This layer is not necessary when using a soil-less compost, otherwise it can consist of gravel, wood charcoal fragments or chippings of expanded polystyrene.

When re-potting, make sure that the new container is not too large. It does not normally need to be more than 2–3 cm (1–1½ in) larger in diameter than the previous one. This should provide ample growing space for at least a year.

Remove the plant from its old pot very carefully, if possible without breaking up the ball of soil surrounding its roots. It is a good idea to make the soil slightly damp half an hour before starting work.

Plants can be re-potted at any time of year, but preferably in the autumn or at the end of the winter.

As a matter of fact, plants prefer to grow in comparatively small pots and if they are planted in pots which are too large, their roots become over-developed. This is detrimental to the leaves and flowers. If a plant cannot conveniently be re-potted, carefully scrape away and remove the top 2 cm (1 in) or so of soil in the pot and replace with fresh soil.

Pruning/Cutting back

Many plants will eventually grow too large for their position or will become thin and leggy. Cut back over-long branches to a lower convenient shoot to induce new growth and create a better shape.

Propagation

Under normal circumstances this should not really be carried out at home but is better left to the experienced nurseryman. However, anyone wishing to try for themselves can follow one of these three techniques:

☐ Layering in June–July.

☐ Taking a cutting and planting it in very sandy soil; cuttings can be taken at any time of year but are generally more successful in the spring.

☐ Growing roots in water by placing a cutting in a transparent vase of water. The water should be replenished as it is absorbed or evaporates, but the level should gradually be allowed to drop. When the roots appear, the young plant can be potted in houseplant compost which can be obtained from a garden centre or florist's shop.

DISEASES

Like all living organisms, plants breathe, eat, grow, move, fall ill and finally die. Plants, then, are sometimes attacked by pathogenic agents which act in different ways, producing a variety of different symptoms. From these symptoms an accurate diagnosis can be made and appropriate remedial action can then be taken.

Why do plants fall ill?

It is not easy to give a precise answer to this question. There are so many reasons. Illness can be caused by animal parasites, fungi or bacteria, or by environmental conditions such as too much or too little light, water, warmth and so on. In the first case we are talking of parasitic disease, in the second of physiological disorder.

With the large number of insecticides and fungicides on the market there should be a marked decline in the incidence of plant disease. In fact, apart from a few disorders which are easy to eliminate, such as rust or pollution, many infections are definitely on the increase, particularly at certain times of the year.

It is not easy to cure a plant once disease has really taken hold. It is therefore better to take preventive measures with appropriate sprays when certain climatic conditions prevail—conditions which are conducive to bacterial, fungal and even insect life.

In this way the plant will be able to combat disease at the first attack. Human beings take similar preventive measures when they resort to influenza vaccinations.

Most of us will have seen the way geraniums 'bolt' when they are kept in a poorly lit spot, and other houseplants wilt and lose their leaves when they are not given enough water. This is due to certain physiological disorders. Here are the most common ones:

Deficiency diseases

These can show themselves in a variety of ways, usually by leaf discolouration, which is caused by some form of nutritional deficiency.

Premature dropping of fruit

In this case, fruit may fall almost as soon as it is formed, or just before ripening. This is usually due to climatic conditions, weakness, insufficient water or pests which have attacked the buds, leaves or flowers of the plant.

1. *Close-up of a geranium leaf attacked by rust. The leaves of the affected plant will have rust-coloured patches and dryness.*

1

2–3. *A small azalea plant attacked by a fungus called* exobasidium rhododendri; *the abnormal growths are the plant's defensive reaction to this kind of fungal attack. This is rarely found with indoor specimens. Neglect and periods of under or overwatering have resulted in root* rot *for the bowl of houseplants below.*
4. *This maidenhair fern appears to be suffering from chlorosis (i.e. insufficient chlorophyll). Note the characteristic yellowing of the foliage.*
5. *An aphelandra which has lost its leaves because of faulty watering and lack of humidity.*

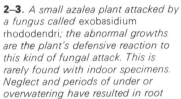

Etiolation

This is not exactly an illness, more a form of temporary weakness as a result of the plant being kept for a long time in poor light. This will cause the chlorophyll to decrease (chlorophyll can only be manufactured in the light), the plant to weaken and the leaves to turn white.

Yellowing leaves

This is one of the commonest signs of ill-health in houseplants and is generally caused by:

- ☐ Overwatering
- ☐ Underwatering
- ☐ Cold draughts
- ☐ Lack of light
- ☐ Chlorosis or lack of iron
- ☐ If chlorosis is diagnosed, an iron-based product can be added to the water and used according to the instructions on the pack.

Although diseases of houseplants are almost without exception physiological in origin, which is to say that they come from some fault in treatment rather than from infection, the main exception is when certain plants are infected by a virus disease which has been transmitted by an attack of insects such as aphids.

When insects of any kind appear on a plant, deal with

them immediately to prevent them from spreading to other plants.

There are several insecticides available as sprays that will destroy several species of insects at once. These should only be used out of doors because they are poisonous. It is also possible to use a pyrethrum-based

PEST RECOGNITION AND TREATMENT

Pest	Appearance	Species attacked	Symptoms	Treatment	When to treat
Aphids Greenfly and blackfly	Small green or black flying insects mainly in clusters on new and tender growth.	Almost any.	Curling and discolouring of shoots and appearance of sticky honeydew.	Spray with any good garden insecticide.	At first sign of attack.
Mealy Bug	A small tuft of white, cotton-wool-like, waxy material in leaf axils or growing shoots. Small reddish insect in centre.	Almost any, especially cacti.	Yellowing of leaves multiplication of woolly tufts.	Spray with malathion at fortnightly intervals or touch tufts with matchstick dipped in methylated spirits.	At first sign of attack.
Red Spider Mite	Tiny mite almost invisible but recognized by fine web on undersides of leaves.	Many, especially vines such as cissus and other multiple-leaved plants.	Dry, brittle leaves, misshapen and discoloured.	Spray three times weekly with derris. Volck or malathion. Prevent attack by increasing humidity, giving plants light sprays with plain water.	At first sign of attack.
Scale	Small, flat insect like a tiny wood-louse sticking firmly to undersides of leaves, etc.	Many.	Appearance of honeydew and a black sooty mould.	Pick off and destroy insects with knife or pin. Spray 2–3 times at 14-day intervals with malathion or equivalent.	At first recognition.
Whitefly	Small white flies feeding both as adults and young on undersides of leaves.	Mainly tender-leaved species.	Mottled and yellowed spotting on upper surface of leaves.	Spray with malathion or lindane.	As soon as recognized.
Thrips	Small dark brown insects on leaves and flowers.	Azaleas, cyclamen and some aroids among others.	Malformed flowers and mottled leaves.	Spray with malathion or lindane twice or so at ten day intervals.	At first sign of attack.
Caterpillars	Various shapes, sizes and colours.	Almost any.	Holes in leaves or whole leaves eaten. Droppings under plant.	Search out and pick off caterpillars or spray with insecticide.	As soon as holes or droppings are seen.
Tarsonemid Mites	Not visible to the naked eye.	Begonias, cyclamen, ivies, saintpaulias, and others.	Brittle and down-curled leaves, malformed flowers.	Dust two or three times at weekly intervals with sulphur or spray with kelthane or an equivalent.	As soon as recognized.

product that is completely harmless to human beings and animals (though deadly to aquarium fish) and can be used indoors.

Fungus and virus diseases

Attacks of fungus or virus diseases almost always come from over-watering. Secondary causes are crowding plants too closely together, providing insufficient ventilation, deprivation of sufficient humidity, or permitting a plant to stand too long in a pool of water.

The various fungus or virus diseases that follow ill treatment of this nature are labelled as mildews, botrytis, wilts or root rots. Attacks are indicated by the appearance of moulds, powders of fungi on stems or foliage. As a general rule if any of these appear the best thing is to discard the plant, get rid of it and replace it with a new and healthy plant. If this is not done, it is probable that the infection will spread to other plants. It is possible sometimes to treat diseased plants with a fungicide such as karathane or by dusting with

flowers of sulphur, but results cannot be assured.

Important to note

As with human beings, healthy plants tend to shrug off attacks from insects or diseases. It follows that if houseplants are well maintained they will either never contract or will quickly recover from illness.

Secondly, it should be understood clearly that all insecticides are necessarily poisonous. They should not be used indoors except under the most careful conditions

where a room can be closed off completely during spraying and then ventilated thoroughly before it is used again. It is always best to spray any plants in the open air. Even insecticides such as derris dust or liquid, said to be safe for human beings and pet animals, will kill pet fish.

If houseplants are inspected regularly it is unlikely that they will suffer any infestation and if they are grown with reasonable care they should never become subject to any physiological ailment.

ARRANGING PLANTS ABOUT THE HOUSE

These days, houseplants can make an important contribution to your interior design. There is an enormous range of plants available, and with a little knowledge one can select the best varieties for certain positions and living conditions within the home. Here are a few suggestions on how to arrange your houseplants for the best decorative effect:

Use your imagination to group plants attractively, selecting foliage or flowering varieties which complement each other. A tall, handsome plant standing by itself can look very dramatic, but avoid little displays of plants all over the house as this kind of arrangement looks untidy and makes the plants more difficult to look after. Colourful, climbing or trailing plants can brighten a dull corner, or grouped on a window-sill can help to hide a dull view.

Try to group your ornamental plants together in one spot, or two to three at the most, in one of the following arrangements:
☐ In a proper jardinière.
☐ On the window-sills, so long as they are not subjected to intense sunlight.
☐ In the corner of a living room.
☐ In a proper indoor flower bed.
☐ On open shelves so that the plants get light from both sides (this open-shelf system also makes an excellent room divider).
☐ Between the double glazing of a window with some large, brightly painted dry branches or rocks; this creates an exotic decoration to contrast with the greyness of a winter's day.
☐ On a series of glass shelves.

In a modern setting
Plants can follow fashions and have a certain 'line' that may not always harmonize with a traditional setting. The following plants are particularly suitable for a modern environment:

Caladium **Dizygotheca** **Platycerium**
Calathea **Gasteria** **Stapelia**
Coleus **Kalanchoe** **Succulent plants**
Croton **Maranta** **Vriesia**
  Pandanus

For shelves
Plants with trailing leaves and branches are very useful for decorating shelves or odd corners of furniture. The following plants are particularly suitable for this purpose:

Ceropegia *Little heart-shaped leaves.*
Columnea *Leaves vary according to species; beautiful flowers.*
Commelina *Pale blue flowers.*
Tradescantia *Purple, silver, white and green leaves.*

For a traditional setting
The following plants go particularly well with antique, sombre furnishings:

Asplenium **Ferns in general** **Palms in general**
Cocos **Fittonia** **Peperomia**
Davallia **Grevillea** **Pilea**
Dieffenbachia **Monstera** **Schefflera**
Fatsia **Nidularium** **Selaginella**

To cover columns or trellis work
A wall or trellis covered in greenery can make a dramatic impact in your home. In such cases, climbing plants are the most suitable:

Cissus *A vine with green leaves.*
Fatshedera *Palmate leaves.*
Philodendron *The 'scandens' species: a trailing plant that can easily be trained up columns or trellises.*
Rhoicissus *Shiny leaved.*
Syngonium *Will not climb to a great height.*
Tetrastigma *Grows very rapidly but requires a lot of light and does not like excessive heat.*

PLANTS WHICH CAN SURVIVE IN POOR LIGHT

In every house there are obviously some corners which are less well lit than others. Most plants require at least six or seven hours of light a day, while a few are able to live in semi-darkness for brief periods without too much damage. The following plants are the most suitable for poorly lit corners:

Aspidistra **Dracaena** **Palms**
Cordyline **Ficus** **Spathiphyllum**

FLOWERING VARIETIES

Many houseplants rely on their luxuriant foliage for their beauty but there are others which flower, mainly during the spring and summer months. Here is a list of flowering houseplants:

Acalypha *Produces long red 'tails'.*
Anthurium *Bright red, pink or white flowers.*
Aphelandra *Curious yellow plumed flowers.*
Billbergia *Bluish-red plumed flowers which may last as long as four weeks.*
Clivia *Bunches of bell-like yellow, orange or red flowers.*
Cuphea *Small red or red and yellow drooping flowers.*
Gloxinia *Produces bell-shaped velvety flowers in a variety of colours.*
Impatiens *Numerous small red, pink or cream flowers.*
African violet *Produces violet, blue or pink flowers.*
Zygocactus *Strange pink or pale pink trumpet-shaped flowers.*

Attractive and functional flower pots
Houseplants can be grown in almost any kind of container but are best in traditional flower pots with drainage holes in the base. These are then fitted into a slightly larger and more decorative container and the space between the two packed with peat or some similar water-absorbent material. This will soak up any excess moisture and the cover pot, without drainage holes, can safely be stood on any polished surface.

Flower containers with their own in-built watering systems can be very useful. These pots have a double base which can be filled with water so that it just touches the soil in which the plant is growing. The roots can then absorb moisture as and when it is needed. Watering becomes a very simple operation with the use of these special pots, as all you have to do is to remember to keep the second base full of water.

There are special glass vases on the market for hydroponic cultivation and these also look most attractive.

SECTION TWO: BULBS

The term 'bulb' here includes corms and tubers and refers to all plants grown from a perennial underground organ which flowers annually. The most popular houseplants grown from bulb are those which can be forced to flower during the winter months; these bulbs must be planted in the autumn.

How to grow forced bulbs

It is important to follow a few basic rules if you want to achieve the best results.

☐ Before planting, be sure that the bulbs are healthy and firm to the touch, especially at the pointed end. The most suitable soil for bulbs is:

☐ Very permeable so that the water does not stagnate and rot the bulbs.

☐ Fine grained and well sieved, with no stones or other impurities.

☐ Not limestone.

☐ Clay and silica, with more silica than clay.

When selecting a container for your bulbs it is as well to bear in mind that a rectangular box approximately 30 cm (12 in) long will hold four bulbs planted in zig-zag fashion, while a round bowl 10–15 cm (4–6 in) in diameter will normally only hold one bulb. Bulbs should be planted at a depth of not more than 10 cm (4 in) depending on type.

Once the bulbs have been planted, the bowls or boxes should be covered with dry leaves or peat and put in a cool, dark place. This is known as the 'plunging' period. When the shoots are a few centimetres high and the leaves and flowers are well in evidence, the bowls can be brought out into the warm and exposed to the light. Bulbs should be watered when necessary during the plunging period and the flowering season. When the plant has finished flowering it should be watered with diminishing frequency until the leaves have completely dried.

Bulb cultivation in water

Besides normal cultivation in soil, it is possible to grow forced bulbs in water in glass jars or special cup-shaped vases with perforated covers (usually for hyacinths); these will then flower in winter instead of spring.

Cultivation on gravel

This is especially suitable for early narcissi which will flower in winter if they are kept at a temperature no lower than 15°C (60°F).

The procedure is as follows: take a wide bowl, not

2

1

3

1. *Foreground: tulips flowering in mid-winter. These bulbs have been forced to bring them into flower earlier than usual.*
2. *Hyacinths can be grown successfully in water in special glass containers.*
3. *These beautiful hyacinths are growing in moist soil.*
4–5. *The diagrams below show the techniques used when planting bulbs on moss (4) and on gravel (5).*
6–7. *Flowering cyclamen of various colours, with glossy or variegated leaves, are among the most popular bulbs (or corms). These plants can be forced in the greenhouse to flower in winter instead of spring.*

more than 6–7 cm (2½ in) deep, and place a layer of coarse sand on the bottom. Closely pack the narcissus bulbs together on the sand; fill up the spaces round the bulbs with fine gravel. Pour water into the bowl until it touches the bottom of the bulbs. The water should always be kept at the same level. The bowl must then be kept for about a month in a place that is cool and dark.

When the shoots have reached a height of about 7 cm (3 in), the bowl can be brought into the house and gradually exposed to the light. Very soon, green leaves and delicately perfumed flowers will appear.

Cultivation in peat or bulb fibre

Tulips, early narcissi and crocuses can be grown in this way. The technique is very similar to that on gravel but a layer of peat or bulb fibre should be placed on top of the layer of coarse sand at the bottom of the bowl (which should be about 10 cm (4 in) deep); the bulbs must be packed closely together to make a colourful mass when they flower.

These bulbs should be looked after in the same way as those grown on gravel. During the plunging period, the peat should be sprayed every three or four days to keep it moist to the touch. When the bowl is brought into the warmth of the house, the peat must be sprayed daily to ensure that the bulbs absorb enough moisture to produce leaves and flowers rapidly.

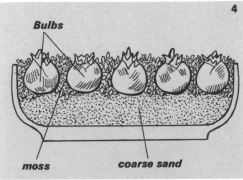

Bulbs

moss   coarse sand

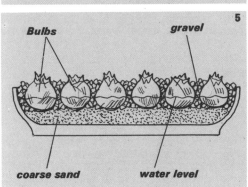

Bulbs   gravel

coarse sand   water level

NARCISSUS

This is the name given to the plant by Hippocrates. It derives from 'narkau', to grow stiff, because of its narcotic properties.

Narcissi are a race of bulb flowers confined to Europe, North Africa and western Asia. The genus differs considerably although the white, yellow and almost red flowers are immediately recognizable. It has been divided for the sake of convenience into eleven divisions. Hybridization in the wild and in gardens has resulted in the widest variations and the numbers of varieties, both past and present, run into many thousands.

Roughly a hundred years ago a few commercial growers began work on the narcissus, raising seedlings and making crosses to obtain new forms and colours. Flowers obtained increased in size and, more markedly, in regularity so that exhibition blooms can be so regular that they might almost have been manufactured. More and more red has been bred into the more normal yellow and the movement towards pink forms has now achieved a measure of success.

Grow them
One of the pleasures of growing narcissi or other bulbs indoors is to watch them develop. This involves planting them as already described and then bringing them into the warmth and light of the living room only when the roots have developed and the flower buds are already showing.

Dig them
All daffodils and other narcissi growing in the garden will be visible long before they come into bloom. It will take at least ten weeks before the young spears grow into flower buds and then flowers and, depending on the weather, anything up to ten days or so before the 'crook-neck' flower bud begins to bend and finally to open.

For this latter period it is worthwhile digging a small clump or two of daffodils and placing them in a pot or other vessel so that they may be brought indoors. The extra heat will bring them into early bloom and although the flowers will not last more than a week or two, the spent bulbs can once more be planted out in the garden to bloom again next spring.

Or buy them
Pots of daffodils and other spring bulb flowers are frequently to be seen in florist shops, street markets, garden stores and even in supermarkets in some districts. They are inexpensive because they have been produced in bulk and they are good value because results are guaranteed. The bulbs can then be planted out in the garden after the flowers have faded and they will grow into normal garden bulb flowers after a year or two.

Narcissi indoors can sometimes be grown in pebbles rather than soil. Make sure the water level never falls too low. On the left, a dracaena.

IDENTIFICATION

Family	Amaryllidaceae.
Genus	Only some 60 species but thousands of cultivars.
Origin	Europe, North Africa and Western Asia.
Type	Flowering plant from tunicated bulb.
Leaves	Long, green, spear-like monocotyledons.
Flowers	Various, but always with central corona or trumpet and surrounding perianth of six petals, white, yellow, reddish or pinkish.
Flowering season	Spring.
Uses	Garden, greenhouse or home decoration.
Position	Indoors, in good light but not direct sunlight.
Soil	Well drained loam, soil-less compost, bulb fibre or with some varieties pebbles, etc.
When to plant	Prepared or pre-cooled bulbs on receipt from supplier; normal bulbs in September for indoor growing.
Propagation	By offsets produced on opposite sides of the bulb.

FLOWERING SPECIES

Most houseplants are grown because of their beautiful foliage but there are a few that are cultivated almost exclusively because of their floral display. The most popular of these are the African violet, the anthurium, the hippeastrum, the cyclamen, the cineraria, the poinsettia, the gloxinia and the billbergia. It is obvious that all these species, so different from each other (some are small trees or shrubs, others herbaceous and others grown from bulbs), need to be looked after in different ways.

Apart from the particular requirements of each plant, there are certain essential rules that apply to all flowering houseplants. Plants that flower in winter are going through the most delicate phase of their annual cycle during the worst time of year, during which they are grown indoors, frequently in an overheated, dry atmosphere, often short of oxygen and polluted by central heating fumes.

The most suitable room temperature at which to keep plants is about 16–18°C (60–65°F). If it is not possible to place the plants in a cool position in the house, we would suggest taking the following measures:

☐ Keep the flower pots in a well lit spot away from direct sunlight.

☐ Place the flower pots on a plate, or group several on a tray containing a layer of peat or gravel that should always be kept moist. In this way, the moisture will evaporate slowly into the heated room, creating a humid atmosphere around the plants which will help to keep them in good condition.

☐ Water the plants more frequently than is usually recommended for each species, using less water than usual. It is most important to make sure that your plant is never thirsty, because even the first hint of dehydration will force it to take defensive action by shedding all its lower leaves and flowers as these are not essential for its survival. The plant will concentrate on saving the uppermost leaves which are vital for the absorption of oxygen.

☐ Bathe the leaves with cotton wool or a soft brush soaked in water. This is particularly important as plants must not be sprayed while they are in flower for fear of damaging their petals. Leaves that are covered in hairs have to be handled with special care as they mark so easily. It is always a good idea to clean only the underside of these leaves as this is often where the pores are to be found; plants with smooth or shiny leaves have pores on the upper side.

1–2. The poinsettia (1) and the azalea (2) are two of the most popular flowering houseplants.

The following pages illustrate the most popular and most beautiful of the many varieties of flowering houseplants.

ACALYPHA

The acalypha is considered to be a symbol of longevity because of its long red 'tails'. It is therefore very suitable as a birthday present, particularly for the more elderly.

The origin of the name 'acalypha' is not known, but it was first used by Hippocrates to mean 'nettle'. Subsequently, for some unknown reason, the name was given to the ornamental plant which we know today. The best known species of acalypha, *A. hispida,* is commonly known as 'fox tail', 'red leaves' and 'copper leaves', 'red hot cat's tail' or 'chenille plant'.

Robust and unpretentious
The acalypha is not an easy plant to find in a florist's shop, which is a pity because it is an unusual plant and does not require too much looking after.

The acalypha must be kept indoors during the winter months; in summer it can go outside provided it is in a shady, sheltered spot, preferably on a terrace or porch. In winter the plant should be kept in a well lit position away from direct sunlight. Excessive heat (over 22°C or 70°F) can cause damage if the soil is not kept cool and moist. Until the red or cream tails appear, the plant should be sprayed with a fine spray two or three times a week.

Prefers a 'snug' plant pot
Like all houseplants, the acalypha does not like to be planted in too large a container. However, this does not mean that you go to the other extreme and cramp its roots.

The acalypha can be repotted when it has stopped flowering and all the tails have fallen off. The new pot should not be much larger than the previous one; as a general rule it need only be 2 cm (1 in) in diameter larger. Flower pots with their own in-built watering systems are especially suitable for this plant (see section on Flower Pots).

Feed the acalypha once a month
The acalypha should be given soluble fertilizer once a month to keep it in good condition. The dose varies from product to product, so it is advisable to give a smaller dose of fertilizer than indicated, and then repeat the operation a week later. In this way there is no danger of 'burning' the plant, or of giving it a violent burst of energy. In summer the acalypha does not need feeding but at the end of September the fertilizer feeding can be started again.

Propagation of the acalypha can be extremely tricky and is best left to experts as it can only successfully be carried out in a greenhouse.

The distinctive red 'tails' of the acalypha are very beautiful, and this houseplant does not need too much care. It can survive in a cool atmosphere, provided that the temperature does not drop below 15°C (60°F).

IDENTIFICATION

Family	*Euphorbiaceae.*
Genus	*Comprises about 200 species.*
Origin	*From various corners of the earth where the climate is tropical or sub-tropical; the most popular species, A. hispida, comes from Java; the A. wilkesiana, which has beautiful coloured leaves, comes from the South Sea Islands.*
Type	*Woody trees 30–50 cm (12–20 in) high.*
Leaves	*Large, oval, deep green in A. hispida; not very large, bronze-green turning to red-purple in the A. wilkesiana.*
Flowers	*Long (up to 50 cm or 20 in) red or cream tails in the A. hispida; short red tails in the A. wilkesiana species.*
Flowering season	*Summer.*
Uses	*As a houseplant; can also be used in hanging baskets or to decorate columns.*
Position	*As for all houseplants, in a well lit position, but not in the sun; it does not like draughts or excessive heat (more than 22°C or 70°F).*
When to plant or to re-pot	*When the flowers have fallen off.*

AECHMEA

The name of this most popular houseplant comes from the Greek 'aechme', or 'point', which refers to the sharp spikes on the long-lasting bracts which protect the little flowers.

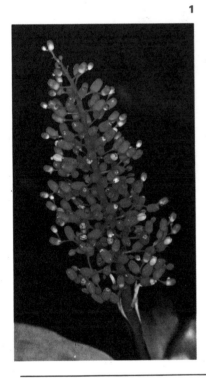

Easy to water

Aechmea plants are happiest in a warm atmosphere and they need a good light but should be kept away from direct sunlight and protected from draughts. The aechmea is of tropical origin and is among the most beautiful of all the houseplants.

Like all bromeliads the aechmea forms a cup or vase at the centre of its stiff leaves and this should be kept filled with water at all times. The soil itself should not be watered at all except once a month or so in summer when giving a light liquid feed. Too wet a soil leads to root rot. The interesting and attractive inflorescence rises on a long stem from the centre of the cup.

1. *Close-up of the* Aechmea fulgens *flower head.*
2. *A group of* Aechmea chantini. *This beautiful houseplant has large flowers of various colours that will* last for several weeks if well looked after and given sufficient light, a constant temperature and little water.

The most decorative species

These are the most decorative aechmea plants:

A. chantini
Red and yellow flowers with brightly banded arching leaves.
A. fulgens
Red and purple flowers.

A. marmorata
Violet-blue flowers on a red scape.
A. rhodocyanea (sometimes known as *A. fasciata* and more rarely as *Billbergia rhodocyanea*)
Blue or violet flowers on a long-lasting pink scape.

IDENTIFICATION

Family	Bromeliaceae.
Genus	About 130 species.
Origin	Tropical America.
Type	Perennial evergreen herbaceous plants about 30–60 cm (12–24 in) high, mainly epiphytic, rarely terrestrial.
Leaves	Linear, curved with spiny edges, fleshy, growing out and up from a central point; generally green or grey-green with lighter or darker stripes.
Flowers	In different shapes and colours according to species, all attractive, some long-lasting.
Flowering season	Normally summer, but can be forced in the greenhouse to flower at most times.
Uses	As a houseplant.
Position	Generally tolerant plants, but prefer a light situation with a temperature of about 15°C (60°F).
Soil	Well drained but rich and fibrous.
When to plant	Aechmeas will not normally need re-potting unless more than one plant is allowed to develop.
Propagation	When a plant has finished flowering, a shoot or sucker normally appears beside it. Cut this off with a portion of root and pot it up to make a new plant.
Feeding	If normal liquid fertilizer is poured into the central cup or vase it may stain the leaves. Better applied as a foliar feed or occasionally to the soil.

ANTHURIUM

1

In its countries of origin, the anthurium is thought to be a magic plant with supernatural powers. It is generally believed that the brightly shining flowers of various colours can rid the house of illness.

The anthurium is also known as 'Flamingo plant' or 'pigtail plant', a beautiful tropical plant that was named in 1829 by the naturalist, Schott. The name anthurium derives from the Greek 'anthos', a 'flower', and 'oura', or 'tail', to describe the flower itself. The brightly coloured spathe surrounds a yellow or white spike-shaped inflorescence in the centre which can be either erect or curled.

The flowering and the non-flowering species

There are two distinct groups available: the so-called 'flowering' species, because of their interesting spathes, and the 'leafy' species, which have magnificent leaves:

Flowering species
A. andreanum
Leaves 20 cm (8 in) long; the spathes are usually bright red and the flowers appear in early spring.
A. scherzerianum
The easiest to keep as a houseplant as it frequently flowers again; it has long spathes of various colours and the flower is a spiral spike.

Leafy species
A. crystallinum
Silvery-white veined leaves about 30 cm (12 in) long and 20–30 cm (8–12 in) wide, and an unobtrusive greenish-violet spathe with an aromatic perfume.
A. veitchii
The most attractive and the least common species. Its leaves are sometimes up to 1 m (39 in) long and 50 cm (20 in) wide; they are heavily veined and corrugated.

2

1–2. The anthurium is particularly suitable for sophisticated plant arrangements because of its beautiful red 'flowers' and green shining leaves.

3. *Here you can see the famous 'corkscrew' flower of the anthurium (*A. scherzianum*).*
4. *The beautiful white spathe of an anthurium hybrid.*

5. *Another group of flowering A. scherzerianum.*

IDENTIFICATION

Family	Araceae.
Genus	According to a recent estimate it comprises about 500 species.
Origin	Tropical and sub-tropical regions of South America.
Type	Perennial herbaceous or woody plant, creeping or climbing, with very decorative leaves.
Leaves	Unusually thick, oval or heart-shaped, rather large, sometimes palmate; dark green streaked with white velvety veins (in the A. crystallinum) or by bluish lights (in the enormous leaves—up to 1 m (39 in) long— of the A. veitchii).
Flowers	Fairly inconspicuous; the spathe, which is often mistaken for the flower itself, is the most remarkable feature of this plant; it can be yellow, red, purple, apple green, deep pink, orange or white.
Flowering season	Anthuriums normally flower in late winter, depending on light and temperature.

Uses	As a houseplant in single pots or grouped together with other plants.
Position	In a well-lit position, away from direct sunlight, radiators and fires; avoid draughts and frequent moves; in a constant temperature, 18–20°C (65°F), this plant does sometimes flower again even in the house; it is not difficult to keep the beautiful leaves in good condition.
Soil	One-third crumbled moss, two-thirds peat and a handful of sand; place a layer of moss at the bottom of the pot to help to keep the roots moist.
When to plant or re-pot	When it has finished flowering.
Propagation	By division at the end of winter for houseplants; by layering or cutting in the greenhouse.
Watering	Keep moist but not wet when in flower and at other times provide enough water to keep the leaves plump and swollen.

AZALEA

In flower language, the azalea symbolizes 'moderation'. Its beautiful blooms, particularly the white ones, are often used in some countries to decorate churches for weddings, christenings and confirmation ceremonies.

1–2. *These azaleas make a really beautiful patch of colour in the middle of the green lawn (1). The smaller azaleas can be used to make a very attractive border (2).*
3. *An azalea in full bloom.*

IDENTIFICATION

Family	Ericacea.
Genus	Or rather, sub-genus, comprises many species and hybrids which are very difficult to define because of the numerous cross-breeds of azaleas and rhododendron. Indoors A. indica *is used.*
Origin	Japan, China, Caucasus.
Type	Shrubby, prolifically flowered.
Leaves	Deciduous (in contrast to rhododendron, which are evergreen), small, oval, sometimes hairy, brown or bright green.
Flowers	Bell-like flowers in groups of two or three, or in large bunches; the colour varies from white to violet, from orange to yellow, pink, purple and red.
Flowering season	Usually outdoors in spring, there are a few late hybrids which flower in summer; A. indica *can be forced in a greenhouse to flower in winter.*
Uses	In the garden azaleas can be attractively used either singly or in groups, on lawns, grassy slopes, beside rockeries or paths.
Position	In semi-shade.
Soil	Sandy, preferably acid, soft and permeable; heathland soil is perfect. If azaleas are planted in the ground, the hole should not be very deep; it is sometimes advisable to replace all the surrounding soil with a suitably acid, peaty type of soil.
When to plant	Late autumn or late winter.
Watering	Should be frequent and in large quantities to keep the soil moist.

4

5

4. *Once the azalea has been moved from the humid atmosphere of the greenhouse into the house, it rapidly loses its leaves if it is not properly watered.*
5. *The magnificent Azalea palestrina.*

The name azalea usually refers to a large number of plants which belong to the rhododendron genus. There is also an azalea genus which comprises only the *A. procumbens*, a small, wild mountain azalea. The azalea used almost exclusively for indoor decoration in winter is *A. indica*.

The many beautiful varieties of azaleas in cultivation have been bred from just a few originals—natives of the United States and of the hilly regions of Asia.

The lowest tolerable temperature for azaleas during the winter is 1–2°C (33–35°F) and during the growth season they should be kept in a night-time temperature of between 13°C (55°F) and 18°C (64°F).

The most beautiful species
It is impossible to name all the hybrids and varieties of azalea (there are more than 1000 listed azaleas and rhododendrons) but here are a few of the most beautiful ones:

R. (Az.) indicum (Rhododendron simsii)
There are about 700 varieties of 1–2 m (3–6 ft) high or smaller if cultivated and forced as a houseplant; the varieties can be of many different colours; the flowers are up to 8 cm (3 in) in diameter.

R. (Az.) obtusum
Dwarf with many branches, not more than 50–60 cm (20–24 in) high with small shiny, almost evergreen leaves. The flowers are small and funnel-shaped, grouped together in twos or threes, pink, orange or bright red. There are many different varieties of this species; Kurume has larger flowers of various colours and the amoenum has tiny flowers only 2 cm ($\frac{3}{4}$ in) in diameter. Kirin is another good houseplant type with small but numerous flowers.

How to look after azaleas in the house
In the house, azaleas all too frequently seem to perish rapidly, losing their leaves after only a few days and inevitably dying shortly afterwards. It is, however, possible to keep these plants for longer and even get them to flower again, providing a few precise rules are observed:

☐ *Azaleas do not like excessive heat,* therefore, if the house is kept very hot and there is nowhere to keep the azalea which does not exceed 15°C (60°F), then there is no hope of the flowers lasting more than two or three days. Similarly, in excessive heat and a dry atmosphere, the shrub itself will not last long.

☐ *They need frequent watering* but in small quantities. It is better to water them twice a day than to overwater the soil or to leave a saucer full of water under the pot.

☐ *Spraying the leaves* helps to keep the plant moist, but there is the risk of damaging the petals. Try to spray only the lower part of the plant.

☐ *When the flowers have fallen,* put the azalea somewhere cool but not cold, water it less frequently and continue to spray the leaves.

☐ *After the beginning of February* a foliar feed may be given once every two or three weeks. This will help the formation of new leaves and buds.

1

4

2

AZALEA —the plant with colour impact

1 Theo Findeisen
2 Petric alba
3 Gallipoli
4 Best Cream
5 Madame Petric

5

3

The pictures on this page show some of the best know species and varieties of azalea, most of which are more suited to outdoor rather than indoor life.

BEGONIA

*Named in honour of
Michel Begon,
1638–1710,
a French governor
of Canada and
a patron of botany.*

Begonia is a genus of more
than 350 species native to all
moist tropical countries except Australia, popular because of the great beauty and
vivid colours of flowers or
foliage and hybridized to produce thousands of named
varieties.

There are three main types
of begonia: fibrous-rooted,
tuberous-rooted and rhizomatous; the last, including
the *B. rex* varieties, grown
more for their striking and
vivid leaves than their sometimes insignificant flowers.

Fibrous-rooted begonia
This is a wide-ranging group
of flowering plants which include the familiar *B. semper-
florens* which, as the name
suggests, can sometimes
bloom almost throughout the
entire year although they are
not hardy and will not withstand frosts. Similar in
appearance are the winter
flowering Gloire de Lorraine
type with their lavish and
colourful blooms, so useful
for indoor culture in the
colder months. The latest
development in this group is
the introduction of the
German Rieger begonias
especially as houseplants,
bred to produce flowers almost all the year round under
the relatively difficult cultural
conditions to be found in
most homes.

Tuberous-rooted begonia
This group of flowering
begonias is probably the best
known and it covers a wide
range from the large flowered
Grandiflora type to the small
and single Multifloras. Most
of the tuberous begonias are
summer flowering but by
growing them under special
greenhouse techniques they
can be produced for the home
to flower at any time of the
year.

Rhizomatous begonia
Probably the easiest to grow
indoors, this group includes
the popular decorative leaved
B. rex varieties, thousands in
number, seldom named and
with colouring which can be
red, white, purple, green,
cream, gold and so silvery as
to look metallic (see section
under *B. rex*). A number of
useful climbing and trailing
species are also included in
this group.

They like humid
conditions
The main reason why some
begonias sometimes fail to
flower well indoors is that
they like a humid climate
around their leaves and
flower buds, yet at the same
time they will not grow well
if the soil in which they
grow is kept too moist. It is
best to stand the pot in which
these plants grow inside a
cover pot containing moist
peat. Water the plant soil
thoroughly so that the peat
is also moistened and then

*Fronted by a B. rex are two examples
of winter flowering begonias: bright
blooms for dark days.*

leave the plant to get almost
dry before repeating the per-
formance.

Good light is essential for
colourful blooms and vivid
leaves, but begonias should
never be placed in full sun.
Tuberous and rhizomatous
begonias will last for many
years with care but the
fibrous-rooted species last
only for a single season.

IDENTIFICATION

Family	*Begoniaceae.*
Genus	*More than 350 species, many thousands of varieties.*
Origin	*All moist tropical regions except Australia.*
Type	*Succulent herbs, sub-shrubs and climbers.*
Leaves	*Alternate, shaped like a lop-sided heart, usually toothed.*
Flowers	*Usually vivid and colourful, large or small, white, pink, red, yellow, sometimes striped or splashed with two colours.*
Flowering season	*Summer and winter flowering types.*
Uses	*In beds, borders, boxes, tubs as well as in pots in the home.*
Position	*With plenty of light available but no direct sun, under conditions of considerable humidity.*
Soil	*Any good potting mixture, including soil-less composts.*
When to plant	*Normally in early spring but dependent on type.*
Propagation	*From seed, tubers or division of rhizomes.*

CHRYSANTHEMUM

The name is derived from the Greek 'chrysos', 'golden', and 'anthos', 'flower', a genus of more than 100 annual or perennial herbs and sub-shrubs coming from most parts of the world.

Chrysanthemums we normally grow in our homes are highly artificial, having been bred to accept special periods of light and dark to give them artificial seasons and having been dwarfed by chemical means to cut their normal height to proportions that fit them into small homes.

After they have been used for home decoration and the flowers have faded, it is possible to divide the several plants in the pot and grow them separately but in order to get good results it may be necessary to 'stop' them by removing some of the growing tips to induce branching. On the whole it is usually better merely to plant them in garden soil and allow them to develop naturally.

Those plants grown for the garden and those for the home are usually sold separately and should be treated differently. Suppliers will advise.

Ancient history
The chrysanthemum is one of our oldest cultivated decorative plants (as opposed to those grown as food or for medical purposes) and its origin is not definitely known, although there are grounds for believing that the Chinese and the Japanese, through many centuries of breeding and selection, gradually altered some of their original species into the types of plants we enjoy today. Certainly the chrysanthemum is a plant particularly adapted to breeding and experiment and, although the normal

Up to a dozen or so flowers top this chrysanthemum plant. They are vivid, bright and of a convenient size for the home.

potted houseplant with its dwarf stems and many flowers differs widely from the large flowered types with their varying flower shapes, it is the latter that are the main interest in chrysanthemum societies in many countries of the world.

Indoor types are simple
The chrysanthemum normally bought for home decoration, probably less than 30 cm (12 in) high and in a 12 cm (5 in) pot, has been specially bred and produced and it requires no special treatment in the home. These plants can be kept for some weeks, attractively in flower, and when the flowers fade the plants should either be discarded or planted out in the garden, where they will almost certainly revert to garden types.

Because they are flowering plants, they will require maximum exposure to light other than direct sunlight and the soil in which they grow should be kept moist at all times, but apart from these two essentials, an occasional feed and perhaps the odd spray over with clean water is all they ask for a surprisingly long life.

IDENTIFICATION

Family	Compositae.
Genus	More than 100 species, many modern types and countless cultivars.
Origin	From Africa, America, Asia and Europe.
Type	Perennial flowering herbs and sub-shrubs.
Leaves	Fleshy, light to dark green, roughly shaped like an oak leaf.
Flowers	House plant varieties usually small, 5–7 cm (2–3 in) across, double, red, orange, yellow, white, in various tints and shades.
Flowering season	All year round for houseplant types.
Uses	As a house plant.
Position	In strong light but out of direct sun except for brief periods.
Soil	Any good, rich potting mixture.
When to plant	Any time.
Propagation	Can be divided and planted out in garden soil but only artificial periods of 'daylight' and 'night' will reproduce the characteristics of the original plant.

CLIVIA

'Lover's tryst' is the meaning of this flower, so the gift of a clivia hints at a secret meeting. Nevertheless, this plant can be given to anyone on any occasion without any particular significance.

1. *The clivia is normally used as a houseplant, but in a warm climate it can successfully be grown outside.*
2. *Close-up of the clivia flower, with the heads grouped together in umbrella-formation at the top of the stalk.*

The name refers to Lady Clive, Duchess of Northumberland, to whom the naturalist Lindley dedicated this plant. The name appeared for the first time in the Botanical Register in the mid-19th century, together with a drawing of the flower.

Beware of the sun

The clivia does not require special treatment except when it is being grown professionally in a nursery; it should be remembered that this plant does not like very hot sun. If the sun's rays touch the wet leaves of the clivia they can be scorched; yellow marks will appear first, then incurable dry patches.

Food and water

Special care should be taken as regards feeding:

☐ Bonemeal can be mixed into the soil when planting (two tablespoonfuls to each pot).

☐ During the period from when the plant stops flowering until the first buds appear, soluble fertilizer may be administered every two weeks when watering.

From April to September the clivia requires plenty of water, but less in autumn and winter. When the plant stops flowering, it is a good idea to give it a rest for two months or so by keeping watering to a minimum so that the soil is not quite dust dry. One final suggestion: when the last flowers have fallen off, cut back the stem to prevent the formation of seeds which would weaken the plant.

The three species
C. gardenii

Leaves up to 60 cm (24 in) long and orange and red flowers 7 cm (3 in) long; flowers in winter. Comes from South Africa and was imported to Europe in 1877.

C. miniata

The most common species: the leaves are up to 60 cm (24 in) long and the flowers 5 cm (2 in) long, of bright scarlet with yellow streaks. Flowers in spring and summer. Comes from Natal and was imported in 1854. Comprises several varieties, including the 'aurea' with yellow flowers, and the 'striata' with variegated leaves. There are many hybrids of this species which are grown professionally and forced to flower in winter for use as houseplants.

C. nobilis

Very rich leaves and flower 'umbrellas' composed of 40–60 yellow and red flower heads; flowers in May. This species comes from South Africa and was the first to be imported to Europe, in 1823.

IDENTIFICATION

Family	Amaryllidaceae.
Genus	Three species.
Origin	Natal, Transvaal and some other regions of South Africa.
Type	A bulbous perennial with evergreen leaves.
Leaves	Ribbon-like, some wider than others, dark green, shiny, growing from the base of the plant in two clumps at either side, widening towards the top.
Flowers	Funnel-shaped, grouped together in umbrella formation on a rigid stem; in varying hues of yellow, orange or red.
Flowering season	In spring and summer, also in winter when forced in a greenhouse.
Uses	As a houseplant, or in the garden; in some favoured parts of the country these plants can be kept in an unheated greenhouse or other light place in winter.
Soil	Garden soil mixed with an equal quantity of leafmould.
When to plant	Re-potting should be carried out when the plant has finished flowering; it is advisable to re-pot the clivia every year, or at least every two years so that it may be sure of fresh soil and rich nutritive elements.
Propagation	When the plant has finished flowering, by division while re-potting, or by cutting away the suckers which form at the side of the parent plant.

COLUMNEA

'Gracefulness' is the meaning of this elegant houseplant. The gift of a columnea can be considered a great compliment.

The columnea is a very beautiful houseplant with trailing stems; the leaves are either shiny or hairy, pale green or bronze-green; the beautiful flowers last for some time. The photograph shows a C. gloriosa which flowers in winter.

Fabius Columna, a patrician who lived from 1567 to 1640 and was the author of an important botanical work published in Naples in 1592, gave his name to this plant.

A splendid collection
The columnea is an easy plant to grow and is extremely attractive, although it is unfortunately not widely known in this country. Marnier Lapostolle had a very famous collection of columnea in his fabulous park at 'The Cedars' on Cap Ferrat, in the south of France. He built a huge greenhouse to house the many species of columnea that he collected on his travels all over the world. When the plants are in flower the greenhouse is a really magnificent sight.

Ideal conditions
The columnea should be kept at a constant temperature between 16 and 20°C (60–68°F). The soil must always be kept moist but not waterlogged, except in winter when it requires less water. Spraying is very important as the columnea likes a humid atmosphere. Once a month it is advisable to use a soluble fertilizer (following the instructions on the pack).

The most beautiful species
C. aurantiaca
Trailing branches and orange flowers that appear in June; comes from Colombia.
C. crassifolia
Stands upright, about 30 cm (12 in) high, and its scarlet flowers with yellow mouth appear in summer; comes from Mexico.
C. glabra
Straight branches; its large scarlet flowers with white stamens appear in April; comes from Costa Rica.
C. gloriosa
One of the most attractive species, with trailing branches up to 60 cm (24 in) long; its large pale red and yellow flowers appear in winter; also comes from Costa Rica.
C. hirsuta
Climbing shrub; purple flowers appear at the end of summer; comes from Jamaica.
C. hirta
Bronze tinted leaves and ver-milion flowers shaded with orange; comes from Central America.
C. kalbreyeriana
Requires a lot of water, even in winter; its branches can be trained up columns or small trellises; the yellow and white flowers appear in February; comes from Colombia.
C. microphylla
Tiny, attractive leaves, not more than 1·5 cm ($\frac{5}{8}$ in) long; bright red and orange flowers shaded with scarlet; comes from Costa Rica.
C. rotundifolia
Trailing branches and rounded leaves; large, long crimson flowers appear in mid-winter; comes from Trinidad.
C. rutilans
Climbing shrub with red and orange flowers which appear in August–September; comes from Jamaica.
C. schiedeana
Beautiful variegated yellow and bronze flowers appear in June; comes from Mexico.
C. tulae
Long, limp branches which can be trained vertically like a climber; bright yellow flowers; comes from the West Indies.

IDENTIFICATION

Family	Gesneriaceae.
Genus	Comprises about 100 species.
Origin	Tropical America.
Type	Perennial evergreen shrubs or herbaceous plants with trailing, upright or climbing branches.
Leaves	Thick, velvety on the underside, shiny, almost varnished on the upper side; the colour varies from dark green to bronze green.
Flowers	Alone or in clusters, very elongated with a corolla which widens at the tip and opens like a mouth; the colour of the petals varies from red to orange and yellow.
Flowering season	At varying times of the year according to species and environment.
Uses	As a houseplant.
Position	In a well-lit spot away from direct sunlight.
Soil	Garden soil mixed in equal parts with peat.
When to plant	After the plant has stopped flowering.
Propagation	By taking a cutting and burying it in moist, sandy soil in a greenhouse or other warm place; the cuttings take root quite easily and it is therefore simple to increase your stock.

EUPHORBIA

The euphorbia E. Pulcherrima, or poinsettia, is a comparatively recent import from Mexico, where its flowers are considered almost sacred. They are used to decorate churches, bridal bedchambers and the nurseries of newborn babies.

1

The Latin name euphorbia comes from Euforbus (the doctor of Juba, king of Mauritania) who, according to legend, discovered poison in the sap of this plant.

The colloquial name 'Christmas star' has been given to this plant in some countries because it is often forced in the greenhouse to flower at Christmas time.

Modern varieties developed in the 1970s are much more tolerant of home conditions than older types.

It needs to rest

The euphorbia is not difficult to grow, but it is almost impossible to produce the large, brightly coloured bracts without giving the plant special conditions such as predetermined periods of light and dark, cool temperatures and a 'buoyant' atmosphere.

Here are some tips on how to look after your euphorbia from Christmas onwards, as this is probably when you would acquire one of these magnificent plants:

☐ The pot should be kept in a well lit position away from direct sunlight, and should be watered in moderation according to room conditions.

☐ When the bracts have fallen off, the euphorbia can still be used as a houseplant as its leaves will remain green and healthy provided the plant is watered regularly. When the leaves have fallen, the stalks should be cut right down so that only a few centimetres remain above the soil. The pot should then be kept in a cool, dark place without water.

☐ At the beginning of May the euphorbia should be re-potted with new soil; it should then be kept in the sun throughout the summer and watered whenever necessary.

☐ At the beginning of October the euphorbia should be put in a greenhouse to form its beautiful bracts; if you do not have access to a greenhouse and the climate is mild, it may be possible to bring your euphorbia into flower under a plastic cloche or home-made cold frame, but it must never receive more than a maximum of ten hours light a day if it is to flower.

☐ The cut flowers (or bracts) of the euphorbia will last for a long time if the sap running from the cut ends of the branches is passed through a candle flame and charred before the stem ends are placed in water.

2

1. *The euphorbia, poinsettia or 'Christmas star' is one of the most popular winter flowering houseplants. It is simple to grow provided that you have somewhere sheltered to keep it during the colder months.*
2. *Close-up of the poinsettia flower head. The little yellow flowers are in the centre, surrounded by red, pink or white bracts.*

IDENTIFICATION

Family	Euphorbiaceae.	**Flowering season**	In a greenhouse, towards the end of December.
Genus	Comprises about 1000 species, of which one is the E. pulcherrima, or poinsettia.	**Uses**	As a houseplant or for cut flowers.
Origin	Mexico.	**Position**	In a very well-lit spot.
Type	Small tree, up to 3 m (10 ft) high.	**Soil**	Ordinary garden soil mixed with one-third sand.
Leaves	Deciduous, a strange oval shape; deep green and velvety.	**When to plant or re-pot**	In May.
Flowers	Small, yellow, grouped together in the middle of a crown of large bracts which can vary in size and are bright red, salmon pink, vermilion or white; the bracts form a single or double 'flower'.	**Propagation**	From a cutting in sandy soil in a greenhouse, but this is best left to experts.

GLOXINIA or SINNINGIA

In flower language, the gloxinia signifies 'admiration'. Native tribes of Brazil use this flower to honour the beauty of their women and their gods. The gift of one of these plants is a token of admiration and friendship

The gloxinia is a lovely flowering plant which can be used as a houseplant, and in some areas is used as a garden plant by burying the entire flower pot in a shaded flower bed.

The name gloxinia is commonly used to describe the sinningia genus (this name comes from Wilhelm Sinning, head gardener at Bonn University in the 19th century).

Gloxinias grow to between 24 cm (10 in) and 26 cm (11 in) in height and their blooms are characterized by their richly varied colouring, ranging through the various shades from blue to purple and from pink to crimson and white. Their foliage has a soft, velvety texture.

Not an easy plant

The gloxinia is not easy to grow as it requires continual care and attention:

☐ The tubers should be planted in March in pots of 12 cm (5 in) diameter, taking care not to cover them with too much soil; use one-third leaf-mould, one-third loam or peat and one-third sand, with added fertilizer. This mixture should be prepared and left to stand well before planting the tubers.

☐ When the tubers have been planted, the pots should be kept in semi-shade, at a temperature of not less than 20°C(68°F); during this phase, the pots need regular watering to keep the soil moist but not waterlogged as the tubers will rot if they are over-watered; it is advisable to add soluble manure to the water every two weeks.

☐ While the plants are flowering they should be in the light, away from direct sunlight, with regular but not excessive watering. Do not let the leaves get wet as they are very delicate and easily spoilt.

☐ When the plant has stopped flowering, watering should be gradually reduced until it has stopped completely; when the leaves have yellowed, lift the tubers and keep them in a box of dry peat in a cool dry place until it is time to plant them again.

The best known sinningia S. speciosa

About 20 cm (8 in) high with beautiful, velvety, fleshy leaves and purple flowers which appear in August. This species comprises numerous hybrids with attractive leaves and large velvety flowers of different colours: white and purple, white and blue, carmine red with silvery markings, blue and violet, pink and purple.

IDENTIFICATION

Family	Gesneriaceae.
Genus	The sinningia genus comprises about 20 species.
Origin	Brazil.
Type	Herbaceous perennials with tubers.
Leaves	In a rosette at the base of the flower stems; fleshy, oval, about 15 cm (6 in) long, nearly always hairy; dark green, velvety.
Flowers	Usually hanging bell-shaped with a very long tubular corolla which is about 10 cm (4 in) in diameter at the opening; the beautiful velvety petals are of various colours.
Flowering season	Summer or autumn and at other times of the year when forced in a greenhouse.
Uses	As a houseplant.
Position	Requires a great deal of light but does not like direct sunshine.
Soil	One-third leafmould, one-third loam or peat, one-third sand.
When to plant	In March in pots of 12 cm (5 in) in diameter.
Propagation	Usually by dividing the tubers; propagation from seed or a cutting can only be carried out in a greenhouse by experts.

HIPPEASTRUM

In flower language the hippeastrum means 'beautiful thoughts of love', a symbolism which is amply justified by the amazing beauty of these plants.

The Latin name, hippeastrum, derives from the Greek, 'hippeus', a 'knight', and 'astron', a 'star'. The reason for this choice of name is not altogether clear. The hippeastrum is still a little known plant and is often confused with amaryllis. It is known colloquially as 'lily of Barbados' and 'Mexican lily'.

How to grow the hippeastrum

If you want your hippeastrum plants to flower, you should observe the following rules:

☐ Plant the bulbs in pots measuring 12–18 cm (5–7 in) in diameter filled with suitable soil (so that the bulb is at least 3 cm (1 in) away from the edge of the pot); one-third of the bulb should be above the soil.

☐ Keep the hippeastrum pots at normal room temperature (20°–23°C or 70°–75°F) in a well lit position away from direct sunlight.

☐ Start watering as soon as the first shoots appear, and then gradually increase the amount of water.

☐ Water the plant every other day; use sufficient water to keep the earth moist but not waterlogged.

☐ Avoid draughts.

☐ Bind the stem to a small stake as the flowers are so heavy that they would bend over if the stem were not properly supported.

☐ When the flowers appear, feed the plant once a week when watering with a weak fertilizer solution; this will ensure that the plant will produce beautiful flowers the following winter.

☐ Move the pot to a cooler position when the plant is in flower; at the same time the amount of water should be reduced, and then stopped altogether at the end of summer when all the leaves have yellowed.

☐ Re-pot the bulbs the following November.

The most attractive species

H. advenum
30 cm (12 in) high, flowers in summer; the flowers are crimson, streaked with green and yellow.

H. pratense
30 cm (12 in) high, flowers in spring with scarlet blooms streaked with yellow.

H. reginae
80 cm (32 in) high, flowers in late spring with scarlet blooms that have white and green middles.

H. vittatum
90 cm (36 in) high, flowers in spring with white blooms shaded with red.

The most common hippeastrum plants are hybrids of many different colours, some with double petals, which flower at varying times of year. Hybrid hippeastrums are available for home growing, some specially prepared for Christmas flowering.

1. The hippeastrum, also known as 'lily of Barbados', is very like the amaryllis. These plants are easy to grow.
2. The flowers, which appear in winter or spring, are the crowning glory of these beautiful houseplants.

IDENTIFICATION

Family	*Amaryllidaceae.*
Genus	*Comprises about 75 species.*
Origin	*Central America.*
Type	*Erect, bulbous plant with hollow stem.*
Leaves	*Ribbon-like with numerous longitudinal veins; dark green in colour.*
Flowers	*Large, strikingly beautiful, usually grouped together at the top of a sturdy central stalk; the flowers of the modern hybrids are enormous, funnel-shaped, in every hue of red with white, yellow or green spots.*
Flowering season	*In winter or early spring.*
Uses	*As a houseplant or for cut flowers; in this country these plants cannot be grown outside, but they are easily grown indoors or in a greenhouse.*
Position	*In the sun or semi-shade.*
Soil	*Three parts garden soil to one part leaf-mould, with the addition of a handful of peat and a handful of sand to every pot.*
When to plant	*In November.*
Propagation	*By dividing the bulbs in the dormant period.*

IMPATIENS (Busy Lizzie)

'I love you sincerely' is the meaning of this delicate plant with its transparent stems. In Africa the Impatiens sultani *is used to make rouge by some tribeswomen.*

The way to keep the impatiens happy and healthy is to make sure that it is never short of water but you have to be careful of root rot. It is therefore important to use a container with good drainage holes. The impatiens must be watered frequently to make sure the soil stays moist. Never leave this plant in a pot holder containing water. The best solution is to grow it in a flower pot with its own in-built water supply, so that it can absorb the water it needs, without its roots sitting in a pool of water.

As a houseplant, the impatiens should be kept in a very well lit position, away from direct sunlight, radiators or fires and well protected from draughts. The best place is probably on a window-sill.

The succulent stems of the impatiens break rather easily so it is advisable to tie them to a stake or trellis when they reach a certain height.

The seeds can be sown in a seed tray during March; re-potting can be carried out at any time as the roots of the impatiens grow in a dense tuft even in water alone and can easily be pulled up without any risk of damage.

The impatiens flowers nearly all year round, providing it is kept in a well lit position, not in the sun, and at a temperature, not less than 16–18°C (60–65°F). Some species can also be attractively grown outside as part of a border, or on their own in the grass; they can also be used to great effect in a rockery.

IDENTIFICATION

Family	Balsaminaceae.
Genus	Comprises about 400–500 species, including the popular I. sultani.
Origin	Asia, Africa, Europe, America.
Type	Annual or perennial herbaceous plants.
Leaves	Oval or spear-shaped, shiny, bright green.
Flowers	Four or five petals with characteristic spurs in the centre; the colour varies from pink to russet.
Flowering season	More or less throughout the year.
Uses	In borders, flower beds, rockeries, tubs or window boxes, or as a houseplant.

Position	In semi-shade or complete shade outside; in a very well lit position away from direct sunlight indoors.
Soil	Rich clay soil mixed with one-third sand.
When to plant	Seedlings grown from seed should be planted out in May; transplanting can be carried out at any time if care is taken.
Propagation	From seed or by taking a cutting, preferably at the end of summer, and planting it in sandy soil or water.

KALANCHOE

1. The beautiful, long lasting flowers of the kalanchoe usually appear in winter, but some species flower in spring or summer. The kalanchoe is usually grown in a greenhouse to be sold as a houseplant.
2. Close-up of the star-shaped flowers of the K. blossfeldiana.

In China, where the kalanchoe grows naturally, it is said that the plants grew from the tears of a goddess in love; for this reason the gift of a bunch of the flowers is regarded as a token of love and devotion.

The name is derived from ancient Chinese and was given to the species by a French botanist called Adanson in 1765.

Be careful when watering the kalanchoe

This plant does not need special care, but you should be very careful when watering it. From May to August it will require a great deal of water, less from September to the end of November and very little in winter.

The kalanchoe can live happily in summer temperatures of between 14 and 19°C (58–66°F), and as low as 10°C (50°F) in winter.

Once it has stopped flowering, the kalanchoe should be severely pruned to give the lower part of the plant enough room to form new shoots. These plants should be re-potted once a year and new ones can be formed from cuttings as indicated in the identification.

The most beautiful species

Among the many species available, we would recommend the following:
K. blossfeldiana
25 cm (10 in) high; bright red flowers in winter.
K. flammea
40 cm (16 in) high; scarlet flowers at the end of winter.
K. grandiflora
50–60 cm (20–24 in) high; yellow flowers.
K. kewensis (hybrid)
Erect; pink flowers.
K. marmorata
50–60 cm (20–24 in) high; white flowers.
K. somaliensis
Erect; white flowers.
K. thyrsiflora
60 cm (24 in) high; yellow flowers clustered together forming a spike.

IDENTIFICATION

Family	Crassulaceae.
Genus	Comprises over 100 species.
Origin	South Africa, Arabia, India, China, tropical Asia and one species only in tropical America.
Appearance	Sub-shrubs, not very tall, 30–40 cm (12–16 in) though some species grow up to 1 m (39 in) in height.
Leaves	Alternate, fleshy, succulent, of varying shapes, with either indented or smooth edges; grey-green or sea-green in colour, with some reddish tinges near the edges.
Flowers	Either star-like or tubular in shape, bunched together at the top of the stem; various colours: yellow, white, pink, salmon pink, pale orange, red or varying hues of purple.
Flowering season	Usually in winter or early spring, but some species can flower at other times depending on the method and place of cultivation.
Uses	As a decorative houseplant; kalanchoes can also be grown outside in a warm, sheltered spot in mild districts; under these conditions they are ideal for decorating rockeries or balconies.
Position	They should be in a sunny position.
Soil	Garden earth mixed with one-third sand and one-third coarse earth containing fragments of stone and a handful of bonemeal to each pot.
How to plant	Species of kalanchoe which flowers in winter should be re-potted in the winter; other species can be re-potted as soon as the buds appear.
Propagation	These plants can be grown from seed but this is really best left to the nurseryman; it is also possible with some species to form a new plant by cutting a shoot from the mother plant between June and August, leaving it out in the sun to dry for two or three days and then potting it in sandy earth.

ORCHIDS

Orchids have been popular for a very long time; some even date back to ancient Greek and Roman times. During the period of the great explorers, when merchants and missionaries undertook adventurous, and often hazardous, journeys all over the world, they often brought back samples of the plants they had found on their travels.

To most people the word orchid has a rich and rarefied ring about it. We associate it with glamour and high living and, indeed, many orchids have a rare and quite spectacular beauty which makes the legend a reality.

But in fact orchids form one of the largest of the flowering plant families. Nobody has succeeded in counting all the different orchids in the world and estimates of the number of different species within the family of the orchidaceae range from 15,000 to 30,000.

In 1764, Linnaeus, the famous Swedish naturalist, identified thirty different species and by 1830 more than 1000 had been identified. In 1880 the number had reached 6000. Today, we know definitely of 600 geni, subdivided into more than 20,000 species and an innumerable quantity of hybrids.

We usually associate orchids with the tropics and although it is true that the most flamboyant specimens are to be found in moist and tropical areas, orchid varieties occur in most parts of the world with the exception of the Polar regions. Some orchid varieties can even thrive in coastal situations where they are subject to the salt spray from the sea. Columbia in tropical America and the Indo-Malaysian region from the Himalayas to New Guinea are probably the world's richest orchid areas.

Orchids owe their name to the Greek philosopher Theophrastus (370–287 BC) who wrote a history of plants. 'Orchid' comes from the Greek word meaning testicle. Theophrastus was struck by the similarity of the tubers of the common European *orchis morio* to testicles. It is this resemblance which at various times has led to the belief that orchids possess aphrodisiac qualities.

Britain possesses a rich and varied orchid flora of about 48 species. All the wild British orchids are of the type called terrestrial, which grow on the ground, whereas most of the exotic ones grow on the branches of other plants, but are not parasitic (these are called epiphytic).

Britain has pioneered orchid cultivation. By 1796—only 65 years after the introduction of the first tropical orchid into Europe—some fifteen tropical specimens were in cultivation at Kew Gardens.

Orchids as houseplants
Which to choose

If you want to grow orchids as houseplants, you must choose one of the following:

☐ Unheated greenhouse orchids, which require an average temperature of 12°C (54°F), with a minimum winter temperature of 8°C (45°F) and a maximum summer temperature of 18°C (65°F); various cypripedium and cymbidium orchids belong to this category.

☐ Warm greenhouse orchids: these require a minimum winter temperature of 13°C (56°F) and a summer maximum of 25–26°C (78°F); the cattleya and oncidium orchids fall into this category

☐ Hothouse orchids: these cannot live in temperatures of less than 18°C (65°F): e.g. vanda and phalaenopsis.

Where to put them

Window-sills are obviously the simplest and best place for orchids; otherwise, open shelving could be used but make sure that the lower plants get enough light. Cane

2

3

4

or metal baskets of orchids can be hung from brackets or chains fixed in the ceiling at either side of a window. The use of a trolley on wheels is very practical as the whole thing can just be wheeled into the kitchen or bathroom for watering, without any risk of damaging the more delicate leaves and flowers.

They need a lot of light

Generally speaking, orchids must have a great deal of light but not direct sunshine. These plants originally grew in the dark forests or in the jungle and flowered in spring when the sun's rays are less strong.

It is not possible to lay down strict rules for the care of orchids, but here are a few suggestions:

☐ In certain northern regions, some orchids can stand in south-facing windows without protection during the winter months (November–March); from May to August it may be advisable occasionally to shade the window with a translucent blind; but in April and September a net curtain is sufficient to shield the orchids from the sun's rays.

☐ In central and southern regions, east-facing windows are preferable and they should be shaded with a light curtain.

Orchids like a very humid atmosphere

The amount of humidity in the atmosphere is just as important to the well-being of the orchid as is the amount of light. With access to a greenhouse this presents few problems, but if this is not available, then a kind of mini-conservatory can be created by shutting off a window bay with a polythene sheet. Inside this little conservatory there should be a controlled humidifier to regulate the amount of moisture in the atmosphere.

If none of these solutions is possible, then one way round the problem is to place the orchids inside a glass tank or aquarium, where it should be possible to reproduce the ideal conditions for many types of orchid.

1. *Tropical orchids can add a touch of elegance to your house, as this picture of the* Cymbidium lowianum *demonstrates.*
2. *Some laeliocattleya hybrids growing in the dead branches of a tree photographed at an indoor exhibition.*
3. *A beautiful arrangement of white laeliocattleya, two pots of* Pandanus utilis, *var. tricolor and some cacti.*
4. *An attractive arrangement of orchids and other houseplants in the moist warmth of a greenhouse.*

The cattleya, one of the classics of the orchid world, has given rise to a large number of beautiful hybrids in the most extraordinary colours. These are essentially greenhouse plants, although enthusiasts may be able to grow some of them in the home for short periods.

1	2		7	8
	3	4	9	10	11
	5	6		12	

1 C. Tenebrule; 2 C. Gasghelliana;
3–4 Laeliocattleya; 5 C. Peter Sander;
6 C. Harold; 7 C. Mandelli;
8 C. Aphrodite; 9 C. Sylvia;
10 C. Rabelay; 11 C. Trianae;
12 C. Heatonensis.

1. *The flowers of some cypripediums are so perfect that they look artificial.*
2. *A lovely group of phalaenopsis.*
3. *A mass of magnificently coloured cymbidium flowers.*

Orchids generally like 45 per cent humidity in winter and up to 90 per cent in the height of summer. An average of 65 per cent will keep most orchids in good condition. A deep saucer of gravel and water under the flower pot is the best way to keep the soil or special orchid compost moist as the water will be drawn up through the sides of the terracotta pot.

The most suitable containers

Wide, shallow terracotta bowls are the most suitable for terrestrial orchids, while the epiphytic type are better off in woven baskets or terracotta pots with holes down the sides so the roots can entwine themselves round the outside of the container. When using a terracotta pot, the drainage hole should be enlarged as much as possible and a layer of stones or terracotta fragments inserted to facilitate drainage and thus make sure the roots will not rot. The pots must be thoroughly washed and treated with an insecticide and fungicide before use.

When a basket is used, the base and sides should be covered with a layer of moss to prevent the soil or compost from falling out. These containers should also be carefully washed and treated with a sterilizing agent before use.

Various types of soil

The composition of the soil varies according to the orchid:

☐ **For terrestrial orchids** the soil should be made up of two parts leafmould, one part fibrous loam and one part fibrous peat.

☐ **For epiphytic orchids** to be grown in a basket, the bottom layer should consist of a mixture of two parts moss and three parts osmunda fern fibre. The osmunda fibre keeps the compost open and aerated, which helps the orchid roots to breathe and facilitates drainage.

Planting and re-potting

As a general rule, planting and re-potting should be carried out immediately after the dormant period (which usually takes place after the flowering season) and just before growth begins again.

This procedure varies according to the type of orchid:

☐ **Epiphytic orchids:** these have 'pseudo bulbs' (green swellings just under the leaves) which should stay above the earth, and rhi-

zomes (fat, fleshy roots). The bottom half of the rhizome should be plunged into the earth, leaving the top half out of the soil. The moss mixture discussed earlier should then be placed round the rhizome. The plant should be supported on a bamboo stake on each side of the main stem.

☐ **Terrestrial orchids** also have fleshy roots, but not all of them have 'pseudo bulbs'. These should be planted in fairly large containers to allow plenty of room for

growth. They are best grown in earthenware pots, not in baskets. The roots must be carefully arranged on the drainage layer and then covered with soil, taking care to keep the plant fairly low in the pot. Arrange a layer of moss on top of the earth as this will help to keep the plant moist and regulate the temperature of the roots.

Do not re-pot orchids too frequently. It is, however, necessary to re-pot every two or three years as the moss and osmunda fibre may eventually

begin to rot or become too compact and the soil will then lose much of its nutritive value.

It is only too easy to break the orchid roots while repotting the plant but do not worry too much about this as the plant will survive. Any damaged roots should be cut off and the injured plant should be given less water for one or two weeks.

Watering is a delicate operation

Watering is one of the most difficult operations and requires great care and attention. The following general rule must be observed: after the flowering season, all orchids go into a longer or shorter dormant period, which in houseplants generally lasts about one month. At the beginning of this period the orchid should be very well watered and then left for at least one week. After a week without water, it should have another good watering and then be left for a further week or so; when growth begins again, the orchid will require more frequent regular watering.

It is difficult to give precise amounts of water because this varies so much from

Some wild orchids, especially alpine varieties, can be grown in the garden or on the balcony without problems.

1. *The beautiful* Calypso borealis *lives in Europe on the edge of the Arctic Circle.*

2–3. *Two attractive varieties of* Orchis sambucina, *which grows wild in the Sila region of Italy.*

1

In Britain, there are various species of wild orchid. All of these grow on the ground whereas the exotic orchids grow on the branches of other plants, although they are not parasitic.

plant to plant. As a general rule the bottom layer of soil should be kept cool and moist.

Orchids probably need watering once a week in winter, twice a week in spring and autumn and every two days in summer, depending on warmth and light.

It is important to use very pure water. Hard tap or drinking water with a high percentage of calcium should not be used: it is preferable, when possible, to use rain water that has been allowed to stand indoors for a day or two.

The temperature of the water is also important. It must be room temperature, never cold.

Feeding
Orchids grown in the house in very rich compost do not require regular doses of fertilizer. But they do need additional nutritives from time to time. Mature organic manure dissolved in warm water or special orchid manures can be used for this purpose.

Types of orchids which can be grown in the house
It is obviously not possible to describe all the orchids which can be grown indoors, so we shall only mention some of the most attractive ones

which can be obtained from orchid specialists and nurseries:

cattleya, brassavola, laelia (epiphytic)
Comprises numerous hybrids and varieties, with large lilac, mauve, white and violet or yellow and violet flowers.

cymbidium (semi-epiphytic)
Very well-known, particularly the miniature variety, easy to grow, flowers are pink, green, green and red, green and yellow, red and chestnut.

cypripedium (terrestrial)
One of the most suitable as a houseplant. Many species, varieties and hybrids can be obtained from nurseries from *C. insigne,* the most common, to *C. dalleeanum* and *C. caudatum var. giganteum,* with its gigantic flowers (18 cm or 7 in. in diameter), which is the rarest and the most difficult to grow.

miltonia (epiphytic)
Also known as 'the thoughtful orchid'; there are some extraordinarily beautiful hybrids which are easy to grow, with flowers of red and white, white with cherry red veins, cream and chestnut brown, wine and yellow, and dark red with white edges.

odontoglossum (epiphytic)
From Mexico with very strange flowers; the most beautiful species is the *O. grande* with huge gold and brown flowers.

paphiopedilum (terrestrial)
Also known as 'slipper orchid'; flowers in winter and is easy to grow. The flowers are chestnut brown and red, chocolate and white, or russet and green.

1–2. Wild orchids appear in many parts of the world, some of them dependent on local bacteria or organisms in the soil or other medium in which the roots grow.

2

PELARGONIUM

The name comes from 'pelargos', a 'stork', because the fruit or seed capsule is similar in appearance to a stork's beak.

Fancy leaved pelargoniums have foliage quite as bright as any flower.

The pelargonium is frequently called a geranium and it is in fact related to these garden plants which also get their common name of 'crane's bill' from a similarity of the seed capsule to the bird's beak.

This is probably the most popular decorative flowering plant in the world, grown everywhere, tolerant even of slight frosts, easy to grow, easy to propagate, with types grown for their flowers, for their leaves and for their perfumes. There are thousands of varieties or cultivars of all types, shapes and colours, with many uses. They can be grown as specimens in pots indoors and out, in beds and borders or in hanging baskets. They can be trained to grow up pillars and as wall coverings. They will grow in full sun and will tolerate harsh conditions of drought, yet their greatest enemy is overwatering. Because of their popularity, pelargoniums have been the subject of much experiment and breeding.

Types
Basically, pelargoniums can be divided into some 15 different types but so much breeding work has been carried out on them over the years that today nearly all the plants we see and use are developed from hybrids and new types appear in different parts of the world every few years, some of them of great importance in the decorative plant world.

In general, the best known types are probably zonal pelargoniums, show, decorative and fancy pelargoniums, ivy-leaf and scented-leaf and regals. In recent years the American Irene varieties have found many friends and the equally new Stellar geraniums from Australia have also been widely accepted. Two small growing, compact types are the deacons and the rosebuds, both excellent for growing indoors. It is possible almost anywhere in the world to have pelargoniums in flower at any time of the year.

Zonal pelargoniums may be identified by the horse-shoe markings on the leaves, which have given them an alternative popular name. They are mainly used for outdoor bedding but will grow easily and rewardingly indoors. Similar are the fancy-leaved pelargoniums, but here the markings on the leaves are almost in the form of a circle rather than a horse-shoe and generally more vivid, with a greater range of colours.

Ivy-leaved pelargoniums, *P. peltatum*, come in more than 200 varieties, all with the characteristic ivy leaf shape to their own foliage and all particularly suited to a climbing or trailing habit, hence useful for growing up a trellis, in hanging baskets, in tubs and window boxes. They make a useful ground cover where heavy frosts do not normally occur.

Regals are identified by their considerably larger flower petals, almost petunia or godetia sized. Foliage is plain green but the flowers usually have two or three colours. Regal pelargoniums will flower indoors for nine or ten months of the year.

Among the scented-leaf types, the flowers take second place, being on the whole somewhat smaller and less significant than with other pelargonium types. But this is made up by the leaf scent, which can be strong enough for leaves sometimes to be used in cooking. Mint, lemon, rose, nutmeg, citron, balsam and peppermint are some of the scents identified.

IDENTIFICATION

Family	Geraniaceae.
Genus	About 230 species.
Origin	Mainly from South Africa.
Type	Erect, trailing, greenhouse and hardy herbaceous, evergreen, shrubby and tuberous-rooted perennials.
Leaves	Usually opposite, entire or much divided, green or colour banded, sometimes scented.
Flowers	Usually with five petals, in umbels, mainly in red, pink, white or purple, with shades and tints of these.
Flowering season	Mainly summer but indoors almost all of the year round.
Uses	Every possible decorative use indoors and out.
Position	Almost any.
Soil	Well drained sandy loam with added leafmould.
When to plant	Spring or early summer.
Propagation	From cuttings in late winter.

PRIMULA OBCONICA

The name primula is a diminutive of 'primus', 'first', probably an allusion to the fact that this is one of the earliest plants to appear each year.

Primula obconica is available in several strong colours and a good plant is constantly in bloom.

P. obconica is merely one of hundreds of primulas and the genus has been divided for convenience into 30 sections, of which this is one. It is one of the best of the primulas for growing in the home because it is sturdy, strong and well coloured but the hairs on the undersides of the leaves can bring out a rash on some people's hands, and for this reason it is treated with some caution.

The basic *P. obconica* species grows only 15–22 cm (6–9 in) tall and the flowers, of a lilac hue, appear in winter and early spring. As a result of breeding work, the flowers have become larger and taller and are now white, pink, red and magenta. Plants are normally easy enough to obtain and with care they will last for several weeks in the house, after which they should be discarded.

Plenty of light

Primulas begin to appear as the days begin to grow longer, a sign that they demand good light. Keep them indoors where the light is strong but where the sun will never stay on them for long. The soil in their pots should never be allowed to dry out and it is advisable for this reason to grow plants in a soil-less compost or in one that is rich in peat or in leaf-mould. Yet at the same time care must be taken to see that plants never stand in a puddle and that the soil is not so wet that the roots drown.

If the soil is rich enough it will probably not be necessary to feed plants during their comparatively short life but a light dose of balanced fertilizer will sometimes act as a tonic to a plant indoors.

IDENTIFICATION

Family	Primulaceae.
Genus	More than 500 species.
Origin	Mainly northern temperate zones.
Type	Greenhouse or hardy perennials, mainly alpines.
Leaves	Radical, simple, entire, toothed or lobed.
Flowers	Varying according to species and varieties.
Flowering season	Mainly winter and early spring.
Uses	Garden, greenhouse and houseplants.
Position	In good light but with no sun and in a cool place.
Soil	Well drained but moisture retentive.
When to plant	Sow seed in June for spring flowering.
Propagation	From seed.

SAINTPAULIA (African Violet)

*'I shall come back'
is the promise of this
flower. In central Africa,
the flowers are used
to decorate tables and
dishes of food at wedding
feasts and funeral receptions.*

Baron Walter von Saint Paul-Illiare of Berlin, who lived from 1860–1910, discovered this plant and named it Saintpaulia. The saintpaulia is commonly known as African violet, Usumbara violet, velvet violet and Kilimanjaro violet.

Watering is very important

The African violet is very simple to grow. Providing it is placed in the right spot and given enough water, it will flower year after year, and your stock can be increased annually by division. The plants should be placed in a well lit position, away from direct sunlight, in a warm (but not too hot) atmosphere where the temperature does not drop below 15°C (60°F). Reduce the frequency and amount of water during the winter to give the plant a chance to rest. The African violet requires frequent watering in the summer to keep the soil moist but not waterlogged.

As with all velvety or hairy-leaved plants, it is not advisable to spray the leaves for fear of marking them, particularly if there is any danger of the leaves catching the sunlight.

The most beautiful species S. ionantha

10 cm (4 in) high, leaves 5 cm (2 in) long, flowers about 2·5 cm (1 in) across. If this species is grown with care, it will flower almost throughout the year.

There are many varieties and hybrids including:

albescens
White and violet flowers.

grandiflora
Enormous, very beautiful flowers.

purpurea
Beautiful violet flowers.

S. tongwensis
Similar to the *S. ionantha* but with longer leaves that are shaded with purple-bronze tints when the leaves reach maturity. The flowers are purple with slightly wrinkled petals.

variegata
Variegated white or yellow leaves.

1–2. *The African violet is one of the most graceful of the small houseplants. It has white, pink, lilac, violet or mauve flowers.*

IDENTIFICATION

Family	Gesneriaceae.	**Flowering season**	In summer, but houseplants or those grown in a greenhouse often flower in winter or at other times of year and can even flower several times in the same year.
Genus	Comprises about six species.		
Origin	Tropical Africa.		
Type	Small perennial herbaceous plant.		
Leaves	Oval, growing from the roots on long stalks, fleshy, with a velvety or hairy surface. The colour varies from dark green to green tinged with bronze.	**Uses**	To decorate the house.
		Position	In a well lit place indoors.
		Soil	A mixture of one-third ordinary soil, one-third leaf mould or peat and one-third sand.
Flowers	Either single or double, very like the ordinary violet, with velvety petals; mauve, violet, pink, white tinged with violet or purple. There is also a variegated form with leaves of yellow or white and green.	**When to plant or re-pot**	This should be done in winter when the plant is dormant, or at least when it is not in flower.
		Propagation	By division or from a cutting, taking a leaf and its stalk and planting it in moist sand or water to take root.

SPATHIPHYLLUM

*In flower language the
spathiphyllum means 'I will protect you', probably with
reference to the spathes which surround
the flowers. The gift of one of these flowers is therefore
of particular significance.*

The Latin name spathiphyllum comes from the Greek 'spathe' and 'phyllon' which means 'leaf' and it describes the white spathe surrounding the flower which looks like a white leaf.

Easy to look after
The spathiphyllum is easy to grow, and if spathiphyllum plants are grouped together, perhaps on a window-sill, at a constant temperature, they will live for a number of years, flowering freely every year, sometimes even several times a year.

The only difficulty lies in the watering: the spathiphyllum requires a great deal of water during the growing season, and much less during the dormant period.

The pot should always be kept moist. This can best be achieved by placing the pot in a second, larger container without drainage holes which always has a little moist peat in it so that the plant need never go thirsty. The leaves need frequent spraying.

The spathiphyllum can be grown in water (hydroponically), or in flower pots with their own in-built water supply. Both these systems ensure that the plant has a constant level of humidity which is essential to the good health of the spathiphyllum.

**The most beautiful species
S. cannifolium**
Leaves 40 cm (16 in) long on stalks 50–60 cm (20–24 in) high; the spathe starts off green and then turns white.
S. commutatum
Leaves 30 cm (12 in) long on stalks 50 cm (20 in) high: the spathes are very beautiful, white, 30 cm (12 in) long.
S. wallisii
The most popular species, has leaves 15–25 cm (6–10 in) long on stalks 12–20 cm (5–8 in) high. Spathes are dark green.

1. The S. wallisii *has very beautiful leaves and the delicate white bracts that are characteristic of this plant.*
2. Close-up of the S. blandum *with its green bracts. This plant grows up to 25 cm (10 in) high.*

IDENTIFICATION

Family	*Araceae.*
Genus	*Comprises about 27 species.*
Origin	*Tropical America and Malaya.*
Type	*Herbaceous perennials.*
Leaves	*Large, oval, shiny, on a long stalk; they are very veined and similar to the spathe which surrounds the flower.*
Flowers	*Small and inconspicuous, yellow, clustered together in a spike which is surrounded by a white, leaf-like spathe.*
Flowering season	*According to species and season.*
Uses	*As a houseplant.*
Position	*In a well lit spot away from direct sunlight, at a constant temperature.*
Soil	*Garden soil mixed with one-third peat and one third sand, with the addition of a handful of powdered charcoal per pot.*
When to plant or re-pot	*When the plant has stopped flowering and is resting.*
Propagation	*By dividing the roots when the plant has stopped flowering.*

TRADESCANTIA

This plant is supposed to symbolize 'wretchedness' because of the incredible rapidity and ease with which it grows, just as misfortunes seem to increase around us in times of trouble.

The Latin name, tradescantia, comes from John Tradescant, the gardener of Charles I, who imported the first tradescantia to Europe from Virginia. This plant is commonly known as 'wandering Jew'. Perhaps its reputation as a symbol of wretchedness derives from its association with Charles whose problems certainly multiplied, culminating in his execution.

How to grow them
This beautiful plant is extremely easy to grow and does not like too much water. It rarely flowers if it is not given sufficient nourishment. Weekly spraying is also helpful, adding foliar feed occasionally. If the stems grow too long it is advisable to cut them back to prevent the plant becoming too 'leggy'. The tips of the branches can be used to form new plants by planting them in very sandy soil or water.

The most decorative species
T. albiflora
Beautiful white flowers and bright green leaves.
T. fluminensis
Frequently confused with *albiflora*, it is the most com-

The tradescantia with its trailing branches is one of the most beautiful and easy-to-grow houseplants. Some species can live outside, providing they are in a shaded position. The various species of this plant have green or purple leaves with small butterfly-shaped flowers.

mon species as a houseplant. Green or green and gold or white leaves, white flowers.
T. velutina
Velvety, pale green leaves and pink flowers.
T. virginiana
Several varieties with pale green to bright violet leaves, and flowers that can be white, dark red, blue, pink, lilac, lavender, pale blue, purple, sky blue or yellow.

IDENTIFICATION

Family	Commelinaceae.
Genus	Comprises about 100 species.
Origin	America.
Type	Perennial herbaceous plants with long, thin vine-like stems.
Leaves	Oval or spear-shaped; colour varies from pale green to purple.
Flowers	Very beautiful but only last one day; very strange shape like a butterfly; colour varies from white to deep blue, navy to purple.
Flowering season	Mostly in summer but sometimes at other times in temperate regions.
Uses	As a houseplant.
Position	In semi-shade.
Soil	Light and substantial, like houseplant compost.
When to plant or re-pot	In spring.
Propagation	By division in spring, or by taking a cutting at any time of the year and planting it in sandy soil or water.

GREEN FOLIAGE HOUSEPLANTS

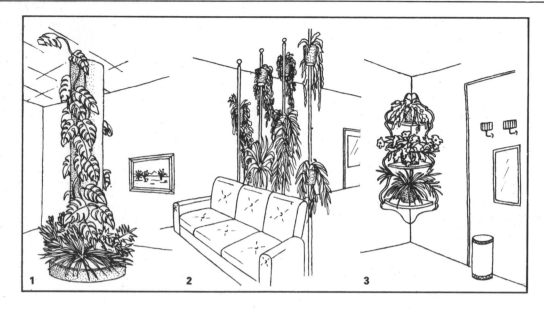

Green foliage species are the most usual and perhaps the easiest houseplants, as most of them have similar requirements.

Obviously, some plants need different care: for example, ferns in general require a great deal of moisture, but the platycerium (a fern) needs much less. On the whole, most green foliage plants need:

☐ Diffused light away from direct sunlight.
☐ Rich, well drained soil.
☐ Constant but not excessive humidity: sufficient to keep the pot cool but not water-logged.
☐ Frequent spraying or at least a moist atmosphere.
☐ Regular feeding (monthly), using a balanced fertilizer.

These requirements should never be neglected. In addition plants do not like:

☐ Cold draughts.
☐ Frequent changes of position or temperature.
☐ Periods of dryness alternating with too much water.
☐ Overwatering, or even worse, being left with the bottom of the pot standing in water for days on end as this prevents the earth from 'breathing'.
☐ Being watered or sprayed with over-cold water.
☐ Being given too much fertilizer, especially if it is close to the stalk as this may burn the plant tissues or damage the roots.
☐ Being re-potted too frequently.
☐ Being in containers that are too large. Plants are usually happier in pots which appear to be rather small in relation to their height. Pots that are too deep will retain too much moisture and may cause the roots to rot. This occurs frequently, particularly with the ficus.

Where to put them
From a purely decorative point of view, green houseplants are best placed against a plain, pale background as

1–2–3. Three excellent ways of arranging green plants in the house, so long as available light is sufficient.

4. Some of the best known green foliage houseplants.

48

patterned wallpapers can greatly detract from the beauty of the plants. Another good idea is to group several plants together in one spot: this will achieve two objectives:

☐ Make them easier to look after.

☐ Provide the same atmosphere for all of the plants.

The pots can be grouped together in a wide, shallow basket, lined with plastic, or in a proper jardinière (in wood, wrought iron or plastic) and placed on a small bench, provided that any excess water can easily be poured away.

Here are some of the most suitable and attractive green foliage houseplants:

5–6. *Picture 5 shows a group of beautiful ferns which are fairly simple to look after; picture 6 shows a group composed of dracaena and various ferns.*

6.

5

ADIANTUM (Maidenhair Fern)

The adiantum means 'love which fears no adversity', perhaps because of the many therapeutic properties of this plant. It is one of the most attractive of all the indoor ferns.

The adiantum needs good light, a humid atmosphere and cool soil. Quick changes in temperature and frequent changes of position are often damaging to this plant.

The Latin name of this plant is derived from the Greek 'adiantos', or 'dry', probably referring to the fact that the adiantum leaves remain dry even when the plant is covered in water.

It needs a great deal of water
The roots of the adiantum must always be kept cool. This plant should be watered every other day. The adiantum likes to be kept in a good light, away from direct sunlight and heat sources. It must not be moved about too much. It should be given a balanced houseplant fertilizer every two months.

They are very attractive
There are many species of ornamental adiantum which are widely used in flower decoration because of their delicate leaves. Here are some of the most attractive species:

A. capillus-veneris
This is the most common species and it is also known as the maidenhair fern.
A. cuneatum
Very widely used as a houseplant and with many varieties.

A. macrophyllum
Tiny bronze or brown leaves.
A. pedatum
Stems that can grow up to 50 cm (20 in) long.
A. rhodophyllum
Beautiful red leaves.
A. rubellum
Red leaves.

Most of these are obtainable only from specialist growers.

IDENTIFICATION

Family	Polipodiaceae.
Genus	Comprises about 200 species.
Origin	Central America, Canada, South Africa, Southern Europe.
Type	Rhizomatous herbaceous plants of various sizes.
Leaves	Delicate and very beautiful, of varying shapes, on long flexible stems; the colour varies from pale green to deep green, lime green, bronze and golden brown.
Flowers	Ferns have no flowers.
Uses	As a houseplant or in the garden, near water; the maidenhair fern (A. capillus-veneris) and the A. pedatum can happily live outside, even in a fairly cold climate; other species must be kept indoors in winter.
Position	In good light, away from direct sunlight.
Soil	Two-thirds ordinary garden soil and one-third peat.
When to plant or re-pot	March.
Propagation	By division at the end of winter; many species reproduce easily from seed.

ANANAS

The name comes from 'nanas', the South American name for the pineapple.

The normal table pineapple is *Ananas comosus*, a terrestrial bromeliad, and it is possible to grow this as a houseplant although it is comparatively dull compared with the more dramatic and colourful *A. bracteatus striatus*, larger, streaked green and gold, yet still capable of bearing a genuine pineapple in the living room.

A. comosus is a drab grey-green with its many leaves in the characteristic bromeliad rosette. It can be grown indoors by cutting the top 1–3 cm (½–1 in) of flesh from the top of a *complete* pineapple fruit (some fruits have the growing tip removed to save freight weight) and anchoring this securely on top of a pot of moist sand or soil-less compost.

The more attractive species *A. bracteatus striatus*, will grow into a large plant in the home with very little care. Its leaves will reach 1 m (39 in) long, green and gold and sometimes with flushes of vivid pink. But these leaves are savagely barbed and dangerously sharp, so make sure that no plant is in a position where it can tear your hands or scratch your eyes, and keep well out of the reach of young children. Both species can be brought to successful flowering with blue or purple blooms and fruiting with a pinkish, tufted cylindrical globe growing from a central stem.

Take care
The ordinary pineapple, *A. comosus,* is easy to grow and makes no demands other than having its rooting medium kept moist. It is a slow grower and for the first few months it will be difficult to decide whether it is growing or not. If it maintains its grey-green appearance it is growing well.

The more exciting *A. bracteatus striatus* should be handled more carefully for it grows into a large plant that may occupy about a cubic metre (1 cubic yard) of space in the home and, because it could cause an injury, it should be kept in a place where contact is unlikely. Care should also be taken that it is grown in a container that will not fall over if shaken.

So long as it has good light, even direct sunlight for brief periods in the day, and a moist root system it will grow well and comparatively quickly indoors. Rather than try to dust the saw-toothed leaves, spray them with clean water to remove any surface dust.

A young Ananas bracteatus striatus or decorative pineapple grows at the back of this group. In front is a pot of calendula flowers and a small growing dracaena.

IDENTIFICATION

Family	Bromeliaceae.
Genus	Only three species.
Origin	Brazil.
Type	Herbaceous perennial terrestrial bromeliads.
Leaves	Rigid, spiny, in basal rosette.
Flowers	In a dense spike, blue or purple.
Flowering season	Spring.
Uses	A. comosus for the commercial production of fruits. A. bracteatus striatus as a greenhouse or house plant.
Position	In good light, even sunlight, preferably though not necessarily warm and humid.
Soil	A mixture of two parts loam, one part sand, one part peat and one part leafmould.
When to plant	Spring.
Propagation	From suckers appearing at the base of the plant or from the growing tufted top of the fruit.

ARAUCARIA

Named after the Araucanos, a tribe in Chile. The best known example of the family is the Chilean pine.

The Norfolk Island pine, Araucaria excelsa, *is in fact a genuine pine tree, delicate in appearance but tough and accommodating indoors.*

A. *araucana* is popularly called the monkey puzzle tree; the species grown for the home is A. *excelsa,* the Norfolk Island pine from the other side of the Pacific near Australia. In its young and immature form it has a fine, lacy and elegant appearance, with grey-green, almost silvery foliage rather like small pine needles and soft to the touch. There are eight to ten varieties of the species.

It is easy to grow indoors

The araucaria is usually sold as a plant no more than 30 cm (12 in) tall, upright, soft but sturdy and of a pleasant glaucous green colour. It needs no staking or support. It is one of the easiest of all houseplants to grow indoors, for it will grow both in strong light including some direct sunlight and in the shade. It will withstand draughts and, although it prefers cool conditions, it will show few signs of distress in a warm room unless the air is dry. The soil should be kept no more than just moist at all times of the year but on hot summer days an occasional spray of clean water over the foliage will be appreciated.

Slow grower

So long as the araucaria is growing in a soil which is rich and well drained it needs only a monthly feed of proprietary houseplant fertilizer. Too much fertilizer will make the plant grow too fast and too soft so that the shoots droop.

If it is going to stand in one position in the home give it a quarter turn once a week so that it will not turn towards the light and lose its attractive symmetry. It is a slow grower and will generally take several years to grow from its original 30 cm (12 in) or so in height to 1 m (39 in) or more but after it reaches this height it will begin to coarsen and toughen and lose its attractive soft appearance.

IDENTIFICATION

Family	Pinaceae.
Genus	About ten species divided into two sections.
Origin	South America, Australia and Pacific Islands.
Type	Evergreen trees.
Leaves	In Columbea section (e.g., A. araucana), long, flat and broad; in Eutassa section (e.g., A. excelsa) awl-shaped, short and curved.
Flowers	Male and female flowers on separate trees.
Flowering season	According to location.
Uses	Decorative houseplant.
Position	Any.
Soil	Fibrous loam with equal parts leafmould and sharp sand.
When to plant	According to season, normally March.
Propagation	By seeds or cuttings.

ASPARAGUS

The name comes from the ancient Greek 'asparagos' and refers to the edible shoot which grows from the root of A. officinalis, not a houseplant but which we all know as the vegetable asparagus. Judging from papyrus pictures and murals discovered in the tombs, the asparagus was eaten by the early Egyptians.

The Romans certainly knew of this delicious vegetable. Cato learnt to grow asparagus, and Pliny talked of the enormous asparagus plants which grew on the sandy beaches near Ravenna and Rome.

During medieval times, the asparagus seems to have disappeared. It was only much later that it was once more grown throughout the world.

The most attractive species
Besides the well-known edible species, which cannot be grown indoors, there are many attractive ornamental asparagus plants. Here are some of the best ones:

A. asparagoides, A. medeoloides, also known as 'smilax'
Very long slender branches covered with dark green feathery hair; it is not easy to keep indoors; it grows well outside provided it is in a damp, shady place.

A. plumosus
This has trailing branches covered with feathery green hairs; it is widely used in cut flower arrangements.

A. sprengeri
Trailing branches and pungent 'false' leaves; this is a popular houseplant and is also used in cut flower arrangements.

A. verticillatus
Can live outside in milder climates provided it is protected in winter; its long flexible branches are useful for covering walls and trellises, and it produces pretty red berries in autumn.

1. *The* A. sprengeri *has drooping branches. It is widely used as an ornamental houseplant and in cut flower arrangements.*
2. *Some of the ornamental species of asparagus produce the most beautiful red berries, but seldom if they are not grown in a greenhouse.*

IDENTIFICATION

Family	Liliaceae.	**Position**	In sunshine for the A. officinalis; asparagus plants grown indoors should be kept in good light, while those grown outside should be kept in the shade in a warm climate, preferably near the sea; the A. verticillatus can happily grow outside in the north.
Genus	Comprises 100 species.		
Origin	Southern Europe, Africa and Asia.		
Type	Herbaceous plants, sometimes climbers or with long flexible stems which can be trained up walls and trellises; some species are shrub-like with woody branches.		
Leaves	The leaves are tiny scales; their function is taken over by 'false' leaves which grow from the base of the leaves themselves and are sometimes spiny.	**Soil**	Must be very permeable so the water can drain rapidly away; asparagus plants generally do not like to be overwatered, particularly the A. officinalis.
Flowers	Inconspicuous, white, in delicate clusters on long stems; some species have scented flowers.	**When to plant**	The 'feet' or roots of the edible asparagus (A. officinalis) should be planted in March or April, the other species can be planted in spring or autumn.
Flowering season	Summer.		
Uses	The A. officinalis is used as a vegetable; the other species are used as ornamental houseplants, garden plants or with cut flowers.	**Propagation**	From seed or by division of the roots, as in the edible asparagus.

ASPIDISTRA

The aspidistra has no special meaning in flower language and is not usually considered suitable as a gift. It is not very highly thought of as an ornamental plant.

These ornamental plants were introduced to Europe at the end of the 18th century by John Bellenden Ker, the English botanist, who brought them back with him from a long journey to China, Japan and the Himalayas. In no time at all, every drawing room and hotel reception area boasted at least one bowl of this robust new plant.

The new variegated forms of aspidistra are quite attractive and, as it is a particularly easy plant to care for, it is ideal for poorly lit and badly ventilated areas where other plants might not survive.

The aspidistra is an easy houseplant. The variegated forms are particularly attractive and go very well with modern furnishings.

IDENTIFICATION

Family	Liliaceae.
Genus	Comprises four species, but in practice only two are grown; the A. lurida (also called A. elatior and A. punctata) and A. typica.
Origin	China, Japan, Himalayas.
Type	Herbaceous perennials with rhizomatous roots and no trunk.
Leaves	Very beautiful, large, leathery, dark green, shiny in most varieties, green and white striped in some of the more special varieties.
Flowers	Inconspicuous. They appear just above the earth line and are blue, violet or ivory in colour.
Flowering season	At the end of summer, but at soil level and very inconspicuous.
Uses	As a houseplant; in a warm climate they can be grown in shade in a garden or terrace.
Soil	A mixture of garden soil with one-quarter peat and one-quarter sand.
When to plant	Outside in spring; indoors at the end of autumn
Propagation	By division at the end of autumn; repotting into a larger container can also be done at the end of autumn.
Feeding	Soluble fertilizer should be administered monthly; it is recommended that the leaves should be sprayed with a foliar feed once a month or so.
Watering	Not too much; potted plants will live for long periods in an over-dry state, but leaves will look more silky if watering is regular and adequate; the leaves can be sprayed with tepid water occasionally to keep them clean.

ASPLENIUM

Like all medicinal plants, the asplenium has an auspicious meaning: evil spirits will stay away if this plant is grown in the garden.

The name comes from the Greek, 'splen', or 'spleen'. In days of old, some species of asplenium were used to cure infections of the spleen and other intestinal disturbances.

It is often called the 'bird's nest fern' because of the shape and formation of its roots.

The A. nidus with its large, wavy leaves is one of the most beautiful species. It is easy to grow, providing the plant is kept in a well lit position away from direct sunlight.

IDENTIFICATION

Family	*Polipodiaceae.*
Genus	*Comprises an indeterminate number of species: some botanists estimate 450 and others 700.*
Origin	*From most parts of the world; a dozen species grow wild in southern Europe, especially in the mountains.*
Type	*Herbaceous ferns, varying from a few centimetres to 1 m (39 in) in height, with creeping rhizomatous roots.*
Leaves	*Very varied in shape: ribbon-shaped and rounded, or deeply incised, indented or smooth.*
Flowers	*Ferns are one of the few flowerless plants.*
Uses	*Mainly for greenhouse culture, but some can be used for rockeries or shaded walls, under trees or near ponds; some species can be used as houseplants.*
Position	*Open air species need shady positions; houseplants need diffused light away from direct sunlight, and a very humid atmosphere but not too hot.*
Soil	*Should be open and moist but well drained; preferably a mixture of peat and sand.*
When to plant	*Out of doors in autumn; indoors at the beginning of winter.*
Propagation	*By division or by transplanting the bulbs which in some species form near the roots.*
Watering	*Always keep moist but not wet; leaves benefit from occasional spraying.*

The indoor asplenium

Many species are suitable for growing in the house. We would particularly recommend the following:

A. bulbiferum
Fronds from 25–50 cm (10–20 in) long and half as wide.

A. fontanum
A hardy miniature species with fronds 8–15 cm (3–6 in) long.

A. nidus
The best known, easiest and most attractive species for growing indoors. This is the popular bird's nest fern.

A. ruta-muraria
Fronds only 2–4 cm (1–2 in) long and almost as broad.

A. trichomanes
The maidenhair spleenwort, with many varieties.

A. viride
Green spleenwort, with 15 cm (6 in) fronds.

All asplenium plants grown indoors need diffused light and a constant temperature. They should be watered daily with very little water, according to size and temperature. The leaves benefit if they can be sprayed daily.

A dose of soluble fertilizer should be given once a month, according to the instructions on the pack.

The *A. nidus* can be successfully grown in water providing it is given plenty of light away from direct sunlight. In fact, this method is particularly suitable for the asplenium as it likes a lot of moisture; the leaves become very bright green, more wavy and larger. You must use very young plants for this as they find it easier to adapt to an aquatic life than older specimens.

CISSUS

The meaning of the cissus is 'faithfulness', but some people also add the word 'gaiety', because it was believed that Bacchus wore a wreath of cissus leaves. The gift of a cissus plant is therefore a promise of faithfulness and a happy future. The name cissus comes from the Greek 'kissos', which is the ancient name for ivy.

1

These plants require watering frequently in small quantities to keep the soil cool; from January to March they only need watering once a week. In autumn, feed the cissus with organic fertilizer, and from March to September give it liquid fertilizer every two weeks.

These plants should be kept in a well lit position, where the temperature never drops below 10°C (55°F), away from draughts and sources of heat.

It is important to choose a suitable support for the cissus to climb up; it absolutely refuses to climb up metal or plastic, or even wood if it is too smooth. The best thing to use is coarse twine or old tree branches with their bark left on.

IDENTIFICATION

Family	Vitaceae.
Genus	Comprises about 200 species and sub-species.
Origin	Australia, central South America, central Africa.
Type	Beautiful climbing plants with slim stems, sometimes hairy, which break easily. They put out tendrils which are easily attached to supports or trellises.
Leaves	Oval, pointed, single or complex, fairly thick leaves; the upper side is in various hues of green, sometimes striped and shiny; the underside is hairy and russet in colour.
Flowers	Small, insignificant, bunched together in an umbrella formation, white or pink.
Uses	As a houseplant; in a very warm climate they can be grown outside on the porch, in the shade of a large tree or on the veranda.
Position	In good light, away from direct sunlight.
Soil	Ordinary houseplant compost or garden soil mixed with one-quarter peat and one-quarter sand.
When to plant or re-pot	Usually in winter.
Propagation	From seed (in the greenhouse) or by layering or taking a cutting in spring and planting it in sand; the tendrils of this plant form roots very rapidly in water and will adapt very easily to an aquatic environment.

The most decorative species

C. antarctica ('kangaroo vine')
From Australia, reaches 5–6 m (16–20 ft) or more in length, with shiny, pale green leaves and insignificant whitish-green flowers in June.

C. discolor
From Java; its leaves are shaded with bronze and silver or white and pink, and it has small yellow flowers; it can grow to a length of 5 m (16 ft). Very beautiful, very difficult to grow.

C. rhombifolia
More generally (and incorrectly) known as *Rhoicissus rhomboidea*. From Central America; has single leaves made up of three leaflets grouped together in a rhomboid form; it grows more slowly than the two preceding species.

2

1. *A cissus plant attractively arranged on a dry root.*
2. *A climbing cissus (C. rhombifolia or Rhoicissus rhomboidea) very quickly creates a green curtain.*

DIEFFENBACHIA

*This beautiful houseplant
has no special meaning in
flower language.
In its countries of origin
the dieffenbachia is considered
the sacred
property of evil spirits
because of its
highly poisonous sap.*

The dieffenbachia has been used to make poisonous draughts to punish criminals, traitors and enemy spies. Spears and arrows are also sometimes tainted with this poison. The dieffenbachia is sometimes popularly known as 'dumb cane' because the sap will cause the tongue to swell and give intense pain if any gets in the mouth.

The Latin name dieffenbachia comes from the 19th-century gardener at Schön-brunn Palace, Austria, J. F. Dieffenbach.

It is easy to look after
The dieffenbachia is easy to look after provided it is in the right place, with good light, away from direct sunshine, draughts or radiators.

It should not be over-watered, as the fleshy tissues of the plant retain a lot of moisture. Generally speaking, once a week should be often enough, but it is im-portant to make sure that any excess water does not remain in the bottom of the pot. Spray the leaves occasionally and provide a foliar feed once a month in summer.

Every two weeks give the plant some balanced fertilizer, except in deepest winter when the plant should be given a chance to rest. Once a year, according to growth, in March, the dieffenbachia should be re-potted into a container slightly larger than its present one.

The most attractive species
The dieffenbachia is a very popular houseplant because of its beautiful, shiny, speckled leaves. These are the most attractive species:
D. bowmanii
Very beautiful wavy-edged leaves.
D. picta
This is the most widely sold

species; it comprises numerous varieties and hybrids.

D. seguine
80 cm to 1 m (32–39 in) high; has also given rise to many hybrids.

The dieffenbachia is one of the most popular houseplants; it is easy to look after and has the most magnificent mottled leaves. It has the appearance of a very thirsty plant because of its fleshy stalks and leaves, but in fact it requires very little water.

IDENTIFICATION

Family	Araceae.
Genus	About 20 species.
Origin	Tropical America.
Type	Perennial evergreen shrub made up of a large fleshy trunk, usually vertical but occasionally horizontal.
Leaves	On long semi-cylindrical fleshy stalks; very large, oval and heavily veined; the colour varies from pale to dark green; with white or contrasting green speckles or blotches.
Flowers	Insignificant, arum-like flowers sometimes appear on mature plants. They are best removed to strengthen the plant.
Uses	As a houseplant.
Position	In good light, away from direct sunlight.
Soil	A mixture of three-parts leafmould to one-part garden soil; the dieffenbachia can also be grown in water in special containers, providing it is given special nutritive pills.
When to plant or re-pot	Annually, not later than the beginning of March.
Propagation	By taking a cutting from the tip of the plant and leaving it to root in a vase of water. When the roots have formed, the plant can either be grown in water or compost. Stem cuttings will root quite easily and quickly.

DIZYGOTHECA

*In the islands
of the Pacific, where this
plant grows wild,
the leaves of the dizygotheca
are thought to be strands of
hair from the head
of the goddess
of love, who has left them
on earth as a good
luck charm for those
in love to
decorate their
bridal chambers.*

The Latin name dizygotheca comes from the Greek, 'dis', or 'two or double', 'zygos', meaning 'yoke' and 'theka', or 'case'.

Once upon a time these plants were classified in the Araliaceae genus, but in 1892 a botanist called N. E. Brown who worked at Kew Gardens decided to group them under their present name.

How to keep it alive
The dizygotheca is not easy to look after. The following precautions must be taken if you want this plant to survive for any length of time:
☐ Keep the plant in a well lit spot, away from direct sunlight, not too near the window (where it could catch cold) and away from radiators and fires.
☐ Do not overwater.
☐ Lightly turn over the top-soil once a year and add fresh soil, check the undersides of the leaves for any sign of red spider mite and take immediate action with an appropriate oil or insecticide if necessary.

**The one species for indoors
D. elegantissima,** also known as *Aralia elegantissima*
Large finely-fingered, serrated leaves on long, drooping stems.

Sometimes mistakenly called Aralia elegantissima, *the Dizygotheca elegantissima is a beautiful houseplant, although it is unfortunately, rather difficult to look after. However, with care it should be possible to keep one alive for several years without it losing too many of its beautiful bronze leaves.*

IDENTIFICATION

Family	*Araliaceae.*
Genus	*Comprises three or four species.*
Origin	*Islands of the Pacific.*
Type	*Ornamental tree-like plants.*
Leaves	*Narrow, serrated leaves, sometimes leathery; the colour varies from dark green to bronze.*
Flowers	*Inconspicuous (plants grown in the home do not usually flower).*
Uses	*As an ornamental houseplant.*

Position	*In good light, away from direct sunlight, in a constant temperature and a humid atmosphere.*
Soil	*Loam or leafmould mixed with one-third sand and one-third peat; there should be a drainage layer of charcoal.*
When to plant or re-pot	*At the end of winter.*
Propagation	*Should only be carried out with great care in the greenhouse; it should be left to experts.*

FATSHEDERA

This plant is a cross between the hedera and the fatsia, and in the language of flowers its rather unpromising name has the romantic meaning of 'lasting friendship' or the promise of 'love without end'. No wonder it is such a popular plant . . .

The Latin name, fatshedera, comes from the two plants which gave rise to this hybrid, the *Fatsia japonica* and the *Herera hibernica*

It needs plenty of indirect light.
The fatshedera does not require much in the way of special care but, like most houseplants, it needs plenty of light (not direct sunlight) and to be kept away from cold draughts and changes in temperature. It must not be too near the radiator or fire, nor should it be moved about too frequently as it would have to make a special effort to turn its leaves towards the new source of light.

It must be watered about once a week, depending on season and size of plant. The leaves benefit from an occasional spray.

It can also be grown in water
This plant can grow very well in water in special containers if it is given suitable nutritive pills. Flower pots with their own in-built water supply are also particularly suitable for the fatshedera.

The fatshedera is one of the most popular houseplants as it is so easy to grow and is very accommodating, even in a poorly lit environment. It can also be successfully grown in water in a suitable glass container.

IDENTIFICATION

Family	Araliaceae.
Genus	None, since this plant is a bigeneric hybrid.
Origin	France, because that is where the hybrid was produced at the beginning of this century.
Type	Evergreen tree with long flexible branches.
Leaves	Palmate, very like ivy, made up of five lobes, 20 cm (8 in) long, dark green, shiny.
Flowers	In umbrella formation; pale green but insignificant and not particularly attractive.

Flowering season	In autumn.
Uses	As a houseplant.
Position	In good light, away from direct sunlight.
Soil	Ordinary houseplant soil.
When to plant or re-pot	At the beginning of winter or in spring.
Propagation	By taking a semi-woody cutting in April or August and planting it in sandy soil under a plastic cloche.

FATSIA

1–2. *The fatsia is usually grown as a houseplant (2), but in certain climates it can also be grown out of doors.*

'I shall tell you of my love' is the meaning of this beautiful plant. This probably derives from the species F. Papyrifera which is used in the East to make fine rice paper.

IDENTIFICATION

Family	*Araliaceae.*
Genus	*Two species.*
Origin	*Japan, China, Taiwan.*
Type	*Evergreen shrub or small tree.*
Leaves	*Very large, bright green, shiny, palmate, made up of five, seven or nine lobes.*
Flowers	*Small, greenish, in umbrella formation, inconspicuous.*
Uses	*As a houseplant; in certain environments (sheltered from sun and wind) it can be grown in outside courtyards, patios or gardens.*
Position	*In good light away from direct sunlight.*
When to plant or re-pot	*In April–May.*
Propagation	*By taking a cutting in spring and planting it in sand, under glass or plastic.*

The Latin name fatsia is the name for the *F. japonica* in Japan. The French botanists chose this name when they discovered that some species had erroneously been attributed to the Aralia genus.

Beware of parasites
As with most houseplants, the fatsia likes plenty of light, but not direct sunlight; avoid cold draughts and moving it about too frequently.

It should be watered about once a week, depending on season and size of plant. The leaves benefit from an occasional spray. During the spring and summer, feed with soluble fertilizer in the water every two to four weeks.

The two species
F. japonica
This is the commonest species: up to 4 m (13 ft) high; the leaves are 15–35 cm (6–14 in) long; there is a variety with green and white variegated leaves.
F. papyrifera
Rarely seen in Europe, but very popular in the East where it can be as tall as 6 m (20 ft); the leaves are 30 cm (12 in) long and can be used to make rice paper.

FERNS

1. The nephrolepis is one of the most beautiful and hardy indoor ferns, with its long feathery fronds.
2. The platycerium or stag's horn is a strange fern which can only survive indoors or in a greenhouse in this country.

In flower language fern means 'sincerity', probably because these plants grow wild in the woods and hedgerows. In some countries ferns are used to decorate dishes of fruit and for garlands at ritual feasts.

There are about 9000 species of fern, from the tiny plants only a few centimetres high to the giant Australian tree ferns which grow up to 25 m (82 ft) high.

How to look after indoor ferns

☐ *The soil* should be one-half peat, one-quarter sand and one-quarter ordinary soil.

☐ *Feeding:* organic fertilizer should be added before planting. Foliar feeds keep fern fronds green and growing.

☐ *Watering:* the soil must be kept moist but not water-logged; do not leave a saucer of water under the pot as the fern roots might 'suffocate': this kind of bath is only satisfactory if it is limited to two hours a day; in this case the plant can absorb the necessary water without risk of asphyxiation. Ferns can successfully be grown in pots with their own in-built water supply. With these containers the roots will be kept moist without the plant sitting in water. Each pot has its own filter which draws in water by capillary action, so there is no danger of the roots rotting.

Propagation
Ferns propagate from seed spores which must be sown in a greenhouse by a specialist. Propagation can also be carried out by division. This should be done at the end of winter before the new shoots begin to form; the roots should be divided carefully into two or three sections.

The best known indoor ferns

Adiantum (Maidenhair fern)
Asplenium
Blechnum
Davallia
Dryopteris
Nephrolepis
Pellaea
Phyllitis
Platycerium (Stag's Horn fern)
Polypodium
Polystichum
Pteris

FICUS

This plant means 'reverence' because in India and other areas of central Asia some types of ficus are grown around temples and the branches are decorated with lanterns and coloured ribbons for ritual ceremonies.

1-2. F. schryveriana *is a tough and easy version of the usual all green rubber plant. A graceful indoor tree is* provided by F. benjamina, *while at its foot lie. variegated trails of* F. radicans.

IDENTIFICATION

Family	Moraceae, the fig.
Genus	Comprises about 600 species.
Origin	North America, Asia and other tropical and sub-tropical areas.
Type	Trees, shrubs or climbers; the tissues release a milky sap which sometimes produces a burning sensation to the touch.
Leaves	Evergreen, alternate, leathery or herbaceous, with more or less pronounced veins, oval, long, with or without separate lobes; the edges are either indented or smooth; they vary in size and in colour from light green to dark green.
Flowers	Inconspicuous.

Uses	As a houseplant
Position	In good light away from direct sunlight in the house; in the garden it should be grown in shade or semi-shade, in a warm, sheltered spot; it will survive in the sun but the leaves will not be so luxuriant.
Soil	For houseplants, use a mixture of one-quarter garden soil, one-half leafmould and one-quarter sand; those grown in the garden should be planted in a well drained spot.
When to plant	Outside at the end of winter; houseplants should be re-potted in spring or autumn.
Propagation	By layering in June or July.

The Latin name, ficus, comes from the Latin 'ficus' or the Greek 'sykon'. Linnaeus or Tournefort are thought to have chosen the name. We consider these to be purely ornamental plants, but in their countries of origin, the indigenous population eat exotic fruits from the *F. carica* (the common fig) and the *F. sycomorus* (Sycomore or Mulberry fig).

How to look after the ficus

The ficus plant is easy to grow but, like all houseplants, it requires regular attention to keep it in good condition. The following rules should be observed:

□ *Position:* a well lit position away from direct sunlight, protected from draughts and heat sources.

□ *Watering:* not too much (overwatering may cause the leaves to turn yellow and drop off); a good method of watering is to put the pot in a basin containing a few centimetres of water for two to three hours, every week or so. In this way, the plant can soak up the necessary quantity of water; another solution is to grow the ficus in special pots with their own in-built water supply.

□ *Spraying the leaves:* this should be done every three or four days; if you want to keep the leaves shiny, they should be sprayed occasionally with leaf shine; this will also act as a disinfectant (remember to stand at least 30 cm or 12 in away from the plant if you are using an aerosol spray).

□ *Feeding:* a compound soluble fertilizer should be applied every month; in autumn it is a good idea to spread a teaspoonful of bonemeal on the top of the soil.

□ *Soil:* the top layer should be turned over very gently every now and again to allow water through more easily.

□ *Check the leaves* frequently for any sign of the brown and white spots of the red spider mite and take immediate

remedial steps if necessary. If, in spite of this treatment, the leaves show signs of dropping off, leaving the lower part of the trunk defoliated, the ficus will have to be layered just below the lowest healthy leaf. Once the roots have formed, the new plant should be severed from the lower part of the trunk and re-potted. With regular watering and care, the new plant should soon begin to throw out new shoots. The ficus may lose something of its normal outline and become more tree-like in shape, but it will look most attractive.

The most attractive species

F. elastica

The *decora* and *variegata* varieties with white and green leaves, and the *doescheri* (with a white, dark green and light green marbled effect).

F. lyrata or pandurata

One of the most beautiful ficus plants with undulating edged, guitar-shaped leaves.

F. macrophylla

With leaves 30 cm (12 in) long and very pronounced veins.

F. pumila (synonym for *F. repens, F. scandens, F. stipulata*)

A climber with tiny leaves which covers walls and trellises like a curtain; the *minima* and the *variegata* variety with white-edged leaves are very attractive; this species of ficus is suitable for cool verandas and humid corners: in a hot or temperate climate, it can even live out of doors provided it is in the shade.

F. radicans

A climber with oblong, oval leaves not more than 5 cm (2 in) long; the *variegata* variety is very beautiful; this plant is very suitable for covering indoor trellises, columns or walls, or for hanging baskets.

F. rubiginosa

The variegated variety is marked with white, like the *F. elastica variegata.*

1–2. *The* F. elastica *is one of the most attractive houseplants.*

HEDERA

This is the ancient Latin name for ivy, and, in spite of the fact that there are only seven species in this genus, there are probably more named varieties of ivies in our homes than of any other houseplant.

1

1–2. *In the comfortable humidity of* **2** *this bathroom* Hedera helix *grows well, climbing the wall and with a little assistance beginning to hold onto the ceiling. It is growing in water alone. On the other side of the bathroom shelf is a plectranthus.* H. canariensis *the Canary Islands ivy, has a larger leaf than* H. helix *and is pleasantly variegated.*

The hedera is popular because no other houseplant is so easy to grow, so rewarding, so tolerant of poor conditions, so **capable** of fulfilling so many roles, so easy to propagate and, finally, no other houseplant will so easily adapt itself to temperate conditions outdoors and grow quite happily in the garden against a wall or up a tree when its days indoors have been completed.

Apart from the popular *H. canariensis*, the Canary Islands ivy, green, gold and grey, nearly all the other houseplant varieties have developed from the one parent, *H. helix*, known as common or English ivy. The suffix 'helix', meaning 'snail', describes the shape of a snail's shell and the corkscrew manner in which the ivy climbs a tree.

Because all the ivies will grow outdoors, it is to be expected that indoors they will like conditions to be cool and ventilated. They will grow quite well in warmer and stuffier situations but there is

a danger that when the air is too dry they will suffer attacks from the red spider mite. This can be cured by spraying with proprietory sprays but it is better to prevent attack by keeping the air around ivies moderately humid by an occasional spray with tepid water.

The range of ivies developed from *Hedera helix* is very wide. Some will have plain green leaves, some green and grey or green and gold or green and white or a mixture of these. Some will grow quickly and some slowly. Some will have leaves 10–15 cm (4–6 in) across and others no more than about 2 cm (1 in). They will appear under a number of varietal names and will then disappear from the market or the stores for some years, later appearing under a different name.

All ivies require much the same treatment. They should be kept cool wherever possible, given humid air or positions where they can enjoy some of the air from outdoors. They improve with

an occasional feed of balanced fertilizer and a spray with tepid water from time to time will both help to keep the leaves clean and to discourage attacks from the red spider mite.

Ivies will grow upwards by themselves if they are given some encouragement. If a trail is laid against a piece of rough barked timber it is likely that the ivy's aerial roots will grow into this. It is

equally likely that in a room which is not too hot and dry an ivy's roots may catch hold of a plain wall-papered wall and pull itself up by this means (see illustration). This can do no more than the most superficial damage.

IDENTIFICATION

Family	Araliaceae.
Genus	Only seven species.
Origin	All are natives only of the northern part of the old world.
Type	Evergreen climbers, by means of aerial roots.
Leaves	Alternate, long-stalked, tough.
Flowers	Small, insignificant, in umbels, bisexual.
Flowering season	According to conditions, probably not at all indoors.
Uses	Outdoors for covering walls, fences, tree stumps, sloping ground, as ground cover; indoors as a decorative climber.
Position	Anywhere, preferably with access to fresh air and if variegated in fairly good light.
Soil	Well drained, gritty loam or a soil-less compost in early stages.
When to plant	Any time.
Propagation	By cuttings.

MONSTERA

*These beautiful plants
with their magnificent leaves
have no particular
meaning in flower language.
In Guatemala,
the participants in certain
religious ceremonies
hold monstera leaves
in their hands
because they
are believed to drive
away evil spirits.*

This plant was named monstera in 1763 by Adanson, the French botanist, no doubt because of its strangely lacerated leaves.

The *Monstera deliciosa*, which is the most common species to be used as a houseplant, produces a banana shaped fruit which tastes something like a pineapple, but unfortunately it will only ripen in a greenhouse in this climate.

How to look after it
The monstera is similar to other green foliage houseplants in its requirements: it likes a lot of light but not direct sunlight. The leaves benefit from a regular light spray with tepid water.

Every two weeks or so the plant should be fed with a balanced houseplant fertilizer to help maintain its luxuriant growth and beautiful colour.

The most beautiful monstera species M. deliciosa
Often mistakenly called *Philodendron pertusum*, it is one of the most magnificent of all the houseplants; it can grow more than 6 m (20 ft) high and its leaves sometimes reach 70 cm (28 in) in diameter; the main stem produces aerial roots which should be trained down the stem into the soil. This will enable the upper part of the plant to absorb the amount of food and moisture it requires.

The Monstera deliciosa, *which is sometimes confused with* Philodendron pertusum, *is one of the more spectacular houseplants. Unlike most houseplants, it needs a slightly larger pot than would seem necessary to produce its striking slashed and holed leaves.*

IDENTIFICATION

Family	Araceae.		ripen and can do so only in a hot climate.
Genus	Comprises about 30 species.	**Uses**	As a house or garden plant; in a warm
Origin	Tropical India and America.		climate it can live outside for several
Type	Evergreen plant with climbing branches		months of the year but it must be brought
	growing from a woody trunk.		indoors for the winter.
Leaves	Growing on long, fleshy stalks; very large	**Position**	In the shade.
	with deep lacerations and oval gashes;	**Soil**	Open and well drained, made up of a
	dark green, waxy and shiny.		mixture of garden soil, one-third peat and
Flowers	The flower spike is cylindrical, surrounded		one-third sand and leaf compost.
	by a fleshy, yellowish spathe.		
Flowering season	In summer, but only in a hot climate or	**When to plant**	In the autumn.
	in the greenhouse.	**or re-pot**	
Fruit	Cylindrical with yellow flesh and a	**Propagation**	By layering or from a cutting; the cutting
	delicious flavour; they take three years to		should then be placed in water to form its
			roots.

PALMS

During the 19th century nearly every drawing-room boasted a jardinière of palms but gradually they gave way to the ficus and the philodendron. Recently they have come back into fashion as they look extremely attractive in a modern setting.

Palms can be grown very successfully in pots with their own in-built water supply.

How to look after them
☐ Keep them in a well lit position away from direct sunlight (palms can live in poor light, but will benefit from strong artificial light for several hours a day).
☐ They should be watered copiously in spring and summer but kept only just moist in winter.
☐ Spray the leaves frequently with clean water.
☐ Feed the plant every month with balanced fertilizer.
☐ Between May and September the palms may be placed outside in a warm sheltered spot. In a suitable position they will greatly benefit from fresh air and the leaves will go a beautiful deep green.

The leaves must be checked regularly for any sign of disease or parasites. Palms are sometimes attacked by red spider mites. These should be dealt with immediately with an appropriate product.

The most beautiful indoor palms
Among all the thousands of plants in existence, some are obviously more suitable than others for cultivation in pots. When plants are grown in pots, they take on a different shape; indoor palms almost lose their trunks altogether and some appear as a clump of leaves sprouting straight out of the earth. Here are the most suitable palms for use as houseplants:

Chamaedorea
A thick clump of leaves of varying shapes; *C. elegans* (correctly *Neanthe elegans*) is the best known variety; *C. pringlei* and *C. geonomiformis* have trailing leaves.

The Howea forsteriana *is one of the most robust and attractive indoor palms. Its leaves should be sprayed frequently and kept scrupulously clean to avoid the tips turning brown.*

Cocos
C. weddeliana, C. flexuosa: with particularly delicate foliage.
Howea
Especially the *H. forsteriana* species.
Phoenix
P. acaulis, P. dactylifera, P. pusilla and *P. roebelinii:* these are all small with drooping leaves growing up to 1 m (39 in) high.

PANDANUS

This plant has no special meaning in flower language, but in its countries of origin (Philippines, Sri Lanka, Hawaii) it is considered sacred because, from time to time, the remains of ancient pagodas or temples have been found among its roots which grow up out of the water like the legs of of a spider.

The pandanus, a sacred plant.

The Latin name, pandanus, comes from the Malay 'pandang', the pandanus is also known as the 'screw pine' because the trunk looks like a corkscrew when mature. It is also known as the 'candelabra plant'.

The Indians eat the shoots of the *P. odoratissimus,* or 'cabbage palm'. In Britain the pandanus is usually grown as a houseplant. It can be grown successfully in a pot with its own in-built water supply which allows it to absorb the amount of moisture it needs.

IDENTIFICATION

Family	*Pandanaceae.*
Genus	*Comprises about 140 species.*
Origin	*Australia, Philippines, Sri Lanka, Hawaii, Malaysia, Africa, India.*
Type	*Upright shrubs or trees.*
Leaves	*Long, narrow, leathery leaves with spiny or serrated edges; they grow out from the trunk in a spiral formation.*
Flowers	*These are insignificant.*
Uses	*As a houseplant or outside in damp ground in a hot climate.*
Position	*In a very well lit spot, away from direct sunlight.*
Soil	*Garden soil mixed with one-third peat and a little powdered charcoal.*
When to plant or re-pot	*At the end of winter.*
Propagation	*By division of the shoots which form at the side of the parent plant; the division should be carried out when the shoots are still very small. They should be removed with care and planted shallowly in individual pots.*

Easy to look after

The pandanus is easily grown provided that it is not moved about too much, that it is correctly watered and that it is kept away from direct sunlight and draughts. It requires a great deal of moisture from April to November, whereas in winter, in the dormant period, it will need scarcely any water at all but the leaves should be sprayed once a week.

Every two weeks during spring and summer, a dose of compound fertilizer should be administered. When the roots grow up out of the earth, the plant does not need a larger pot. This curious root formation is an attractive feature of the pandanus.

The most attractive species

P. lindenii
Leaves growing in thick clusters, often edged with white and very shiny.

P. pygmaeus
Only 60 cm (24 in) high and one of the most suitable as a houseplant.

P. sanderi
Striped yellow and green leaves.

P. veitchii
Bright green leaves up to 60 cm (24 in) long, with very spiny silvery white edges.

PHILODENDRON

In its countries of origin the philodendron is thought to have a religious significance. It has a vine-like structure and can climb up other plants; because of this it is thought that it can reach up to the gods and offer them prayers and promises from the world of mortals below.

The Latin name, philodendron (given by Schott), comes from two Greek words: 'phileo', 'to love', and 'dendron', 'tree', in reference to the climbing nature of some of the species.

The philodendron has been widely used as a houseplant in Europe for more than a century. In times gone by, it could only be used in a heated conservatory or winter garden, but today, thanks to central heating, many species can easily be grown in most homes.

A constant level of humidity

Like most tropical plants, the philodendron likes a constant high level of humidity, but

1. *The philodendron* (P. scandens) *is one of our most accommodating houseplants and is also suitable for poorly lit areas of the house. It grows well in water. If you want your plant to grow vertically, it can be trained up a moss-covered stake which should be kept moist. The picture shows how the philodendron can be re-potted.*
2. *A philodendron grown in water. This technique eliminates watering problems and helps to keep the plant in good condition.*

take care not to let the roots become waterlogged. In spite of this, one of the easiest ways to grow some species of this plant is in water, as it rapidly becomes accustomed to absorb just the right amount of moisture for its needs.

The philodendron needs regular watering, preferably by putting the container in a basin containing a few centimetres of water for two to three hours. If this is not possible, it will usually require more water than normal, according to size, season and species or variety.

So far as feeding is concerned, here are a few general rules:

☐ In November: gently turn over the topsoil and cover it with a little bonemeal.
☐ From April–October: administer a soluble fertilizer every two weeks or so.

The leaves can be treated every two weeks with a leaf polish. These aerosol sprays usually contain a disinfectant (it is advisable to stand at least 30 cm or 12 in away from the plant so that the spray will not be quite so cold when it comes into contact with the leaves).

If the philodendron is attacked by the red spider mite (with white or brown

spots, especially along the veins on the underside of the leaves) immediate action should be taken with an appropriate product.

The most beautiful species

The plant which is commonly known as the *P. pertusum*, with huge palmate leaves studded with large holes, is in fact the *Monstera deliciosa* (see page 65).

P. andreanum
Very like the *Anthurium cristallinum*, with long heart-shaped trailing leaves which are a metallic green in colour.
P. bipinnatifidum
A short stem; the leaves are almost circular, up to 60 cm (24 in) in length and width.
P. giganteum
A climber with rounded leaves which have slightly wavy edges.
P. hastatum
A climber with long triangular leaves.
P. sanguineum
Long pointed triangular leaves that have reddish undersides.
P. scandens
A climber with small, heart-shaped leaves.
P. selloum
Large, deeply incised leaves, with long stalks growing

from the base in a compact round cluster; this species has many varieties and hybrids.

P. speciosum
Large, bright green triangular leaves.

P. verrucosum
A fairly rare species, but one one of the most beautiful; it is a climber with silky, pale green and grey leaves, with brown striped undersides and curled edges.

1

2

1–2. The philodendron (P. scandens (left) and P. hastatum (right)) can grow to a remarkable height and create an impressive decorative feature in a living room. These species are simple to look after and, with a little care, they will survive for several years.

IDENTIFICATION

Family	Araceae.
Genus	Comprises about 120 species.
Origin	Tropical regions of America, i.e. Brazil, Colombia, Martinique, Guyana.
Type	Herbaceous climbing plants or shrubs, with a very long stem which in some species puts out aerial roots.
Leaves	Mainly large, far apart, varying in shape: long, oval, sometimes divided with indented or smooth edges; in various hues of green, sometimes variegated with white; often russet or purple on the underside; some species do not have the characteristic climbing stem and the leaves seem to grow straight out of the ground.
Flowers	Inconspicuous, clustered in a spike, surrounded by a papery spathe which is sometimes heavily scented and coloured white, red or yellow.
Flowering season	Rare and hard to predict in houseplants, as it depends on so many factors: age, amount of light, heat, etc
Fruit	Fleshy berries which only ripen in the greenhouse or countries of origin.
Uses	As a houseplant.
Position	In good light, away from direct sunlight.
Soil	A mixture of one-quarter garden soil, one-half leafmould and one-quarter sand.
When to plant or re-pot	Autumn or spring.
Propagation	By taking a stem cutting and burying it in sand, in the shade, preferably under a plastic cloche; the head of the plant can also be cut off and planted in this way if the lower part of the stem loses its leaves; the lower part of the stem can then be divided into several short pieces and planted to form new stock; cuttings can also be grown in water in special containers.

PLATYCERIUM

*This strange plant
has no special meaning in
flower language.
In some parts of Malacca
and Peru, the indigenous
people make a cult of these
plants, which attach
themselves to the back
of trees; local superstition
has it that they are friendly
gods keeping watch
over the forest.
Perhaps this is why we,
in Europe, believe that
platycerium brings good luck.*

The Latin name, platycerium, comes from the Greek 'platys', or 'flat', and 'keras', a 'horn', to indicate the strange leaf formation which resembles a stag's horn. In fact the platycerium is commonly known as the stag's horn fern or elk's horn fern.

Difficult to water
The platycerium is a very easy plant to look after, which is fortunate as it is most attractive. The only problem lies in watering, all the more so if the plant is grown on a piece of cork with its roots covered in moss; in this case, the moss must be sprayed every day so that the plant can absorb moisture without its roots becoming waterlogged.

If the platycerium is planted in a pot in ordinary soil or peat, or moss and peat, it is advisable to immerse the pot in water for about an hour every five or six days. Or it can be watered over the soil in the normal manner.

The platycerium does not like being moved about, so it is a good idea to put it in a position away from draughts and open windows where it can remain undisturbed. In the warm weather, the pot should be put outside, possibly under a tree, in a shaded but light position, but only if winds are light and the situation is protected.

The easiest species to grow
P. bifurcatum
(or *P. alicorne*)
Fertile fronds which look like a stag's antlers, covered in a soft down. The barren fronds form a rounded ball, first green and then brown, over the pot or roots.
P. grande
Very similar to the previous species, but with broader fronds, normally too large for indoor culture.

The platycerium is one of the strangest looking ferns. It is widely used as a houseplant, often in hanging baskets or growing from a piece of bark or cork.

P. hillii
The upper leaves are split up at the point into a feathery fan.
P. wallichii
Rather different from the other species; the fertile leaves are drooping and divided into only two sections.

Only **P. bifurcatum** is normally seen as a houseplant.

IDENTIFICATION

Family	Polipodiaceae.
Genus	Comprises about seven species.
Origin	China, Malacca, Australia, Peru and Africa.
Type	Epiphytic ferns.
Fronds	Of two types: the young barren fronds grow round the base of the plant in a rosette and are rounded with a frilly edge; the more mature fertile fronds grow from the centre of the lower rosette; they are long and flat and divided up into many irregular fronds; they are grey-green in colour.
Uses	As a houseplant.
Soil	Peat mixed with sphagnum moss.
Position	In a well lit warm position away from direct sunlight.
When to plant or transplant	At the end of winter.
Propagation	In spring, by breaking off the new plants which form at the side of the parent plant, except P. grande which must be propagated by means of spores, a somewhat lengthy process.

SANSEVIERIA

'You are bound to me'
is the meaning of this
plant, probably because in its
countries of origin,
particularly Guinea,
the leaves of some species
are used to make string
and rope. In some areas
of Africa, the sansevieria
is grown near the house
because it is thought
to drive away
evil spirits.

The Latin name, sansevieria, comes from the 18th-century Prince of Sanseviero, Raimond di Sansgrio.

Take care when watering
The sansevieria is one of the easiest houseplants to grow, but it does require care when watering. The following routine will produce excellent results:

☐ Water once a week in summer, by half immersing the pot in water for about 30 minutes; in winter this should only be done every month or so to avoid the risk of rotting the roots, which often hap-

pens with these plants. Feed the plant every month with a compound fertilizer. Lightly loosen the topsoil fairly frequently to prevent a crust forming.

The most beautiful species
S. cylindrica
Tall cylindrical leaves, 1 m (39 in) high.
S. grandis
Leaves over 1 m (39 in) high, bright green in colour, with paler lateral stripes and bronze edges.
S. kirkii
Leaves 60–70 cm (24–28 in) high, edged with reddish-bronze.

S. longiflora
Fleshy leaves 30–50 cm (12–20 in) high with white marks and red edges.
S. trifasciata
The most common species; it has pointed leaves 30–90 cm (12–35 in) long, striped with dark green. The *laurentii* variety has scented flowers in suitable seasons and has

The sansevieria is one of our most popular houseplants; it likes plenty of light, even direct sun at times, and must be kept almost dry in winter.

white or gold lateral stripes.
S. zeylanica
Leaves 30–60 cm (12–24 in) long with white lateral stripes; its flowers are scented, especially at night.

IDENTIFICATION

Family	Liliaceae.		**Flowering season**	In spring or summer according to the general environment.
Genus	Comprises about 50 species.			
Origin	Tropical and central Africa, Southeast Asia.		**Uses**	As an ornamental houseplant.
Type	Herbaceous perennials with rhizomatous roots.		**Position**	In the light, even in direct sunlight.
			Soil	Well-sieved garden soil with equal parts of leaf compost and sand.
Leaves	Growing up round the root, thick and fibrous, sword-shaped, elongated or cylindrical, varying in length, they are coloured bright green, marked with white or dark green, or with paler lateral stripes.		**When to plant or re-pot**	During February and March, before the new shoots start to form.
			Propagation	By division during February and March, or by taking a leaf cutting about 8 cm (3 in) long and burying it in very sandy soil in the greenhouse.
Flowers	Very small, growing in a spike, greenish-white, powerfully scented, appearing in temperate climates only in certain favourable seasons.			

SCHEFFLERA

'Your very presence sets me on fire' is the meaning of this easy, resilient but little-known houseplant.

The Latin name was given to this plant by J. C. Scheffler, the naturalist from Danzig. It was only introduced to Europe in the 18th century and even today it is often confused with the Aralia genus.

Watering is the only problem
The schefflera is not a difficult plant to look after (it has very similar needs to the *Fatsia japonica*). It is, however, rather delicate as far as watering is concerned. It will not survive a dry atmosphere but the roots rot rather easily if they are overwatered. For this reason, the best way to grow a schefflera is either in water in a special container, or in a flower pot with its own in-built water supply. Always keep this plant in a very well lit position, away from direct sunlight.

The most attractive species
S. actinophylla
Known as the umbrella tree, probably the best known species.
S. digitata
A small tree with digitate leaves of about 15 cm (6 in) in length.

The schefflera is a beautiful, easy-to-grow houseplant that will adapt to any environment providing it is light and humid. It requires frequent feeding and likes to be planted in open soil.

S. venulosa erythrostachys
A beautiful little tree, occasionally a climber, with solid, pointed leaves.

IDENTIFICATION

Family	Araliaceae.
Genus	Comprises about 150 species.
Origin	New Zealand, Java, India, East Asia and Fiji Islands.
Type	Small trees or shrubs.
Leaves	Nearly always evergreen, palmate or digitate, sometimes single; shiny and dark green.
Flowers	Fairly inconspicuous, in clusters, greenish.
Flowering season	At various times of the year, according to the general environment and temperature.
Uses	As a houseplant or to decorate a winter garden or shaded courtyard in a hot climate.
Position	In good light, away from direct sunlight.
Soil	A mixture of ordinary soil with one-third peat and one-sixth sand.
When to plant or re-pot	At the end of winter.
Propagation	By taking a cutting in April or by layering in June.

SELAGINELLA

*The gift of a selaginella plant to a loved
one means 'I will love you even after death'.
This undoubtedly refers to the S. lepidophylla species
(known as 'resurrection club moss') which folds
its outer branches over the inner ones during a dry
summer and looks like an apparently dead ball of moss;
as soon as it is watered, it springs to life again.*

The Latin name selaginella is the diminutive of selago, the ancient name for the licopodi plants which are very similar to the selaginella.

Spraying is very important

The selaginella, which grows wild in the mountains beside rivers and rocks, does not like very damp soil, but should have a humid atmosphere. Feed the selaginella once a month with a balanced house-plant fertilizer.

The selaginella does not like the sun either but likes a well lit position: it is not happy in excessive heat or frost, even though the *S. helvetica* lives virtually on the snow line at 1500–2000 m (5000–6500 ft) altitude. Generally speaking, its requirements are very similar to those of the ferns.

The most beautiful species

S. albo-nitens
A species with pale green and white stems.

S. caulescens
Numerous attractive varieties; the leaves, all with a maximum length of 30 cm (12 in), are bright or dark green.

S. lepidophylla
Fan-shaped coral-like leaves, bronze in colour, clustered together in a ball.

S. martensii
Upright or creeping stems and bright green leaves which resemble miniature conifers; there are many varieties, the best known of which are: *ascendens, divaricata, formosa,* the variegated *robusta* and *stolonifera.*

S. plumosa
15 cm (6 in) high with deep green, feathery leaves.

These beautiful little plants are ideal for rockeries and can also be grown in pots or in a bottle garden. They are easy to grow provided that they are in a shady position, on soft, well fertilized soil.

IDENTIFICATION

Family	Selaginellaceae.	**Uses**	For rockeries, winter gardens or in a pot or bottle garden.
Genus	Comprises about 700 species.		
Origin	Europe, central Africa, tropical America, South America, Australia.	**Position**	In a well lit position but not in direct sunlight.
Type	Upright or climbing plants, sometimes similar to moss in appearance.	**Soil**	Must be soft, rich in organic matter and mixed with one-sixth sand and one-third peat.
Leaves	Like little scales, growing spirally along the stems; bright green in colour.	**When to plant**	At any time of the year.
Flowers	As a fern the selaginellaceae has no flowers.	**Propagation**	By division.

SOLANUM (Winter Cherry)

This beautiful plant means 'lasting friendship', probably because the berries last for a long time, often throughout the winter months.

The winter cherry makes a splendid houseplant. It is a small shrub but it has the great virtue of keeping its red berries throughout the winter.

The winter cherry's Latin name, solanum, comes from the word 'solanem', probably South American in origin, which means 'consolation'. This refers to the medicinal properties of this plant, particularly its sedative property.

It is easy to grow

The solanum should be fed in the spring with bonemeal, and it should be given fortnightly doses of a soluble fertilizer from March to September. This will ensure that the plant produces a large amount of blossom. It requires frequent watering with a small quantity of water to avoid making the earth waterlogged.

The solanum does not normally need pruning, but if you wish to re-shape your plant, this should be carried out at the end of the winter before it begins to flower.

From April to October the solanum may be kept outside in a sheltered position but it must be brought indoors at

The winter cherry is a firm favourite because of its attractive berries.

the first sign of cold weather. Indoors, it should be placed in a well lit, airy position where the temperature is not too high. Do be careful not to overwater this plant in winter.

Only two species

The colloquial name 'winter cherry' usually refers to these two species:

S. capsicastrum
From Brazil and Madeira, a small tree not more than 60–70 cm (24–28 in) high, with bright fruits the size of a walnut.

S. pseudocapsicum
A small shrub up to 1 m (39 in) high, does not like the cold; covered with red and yellow fruits the size of cherries in autumn; the dwarf variety, *nanum*, is very beautiful. It is also known as the 'Jerusalem cherry'.

IDENTIFICATION

Family	Solanaceae.	**Uses**	As a houseplant.
Genus	Comprises more than 900 species.	**Position**	Outside in sunshine during the warm
Origin	South America: a few species come from Asia, Africa and Europe.		weather; indoors from autumn to spring in a well lit position.
Type	Small compact shrubs with many branches.	**Soil**	Open, sandy, permeable soil.
Leaves	Oval, shiny, bright green.	**When to plant**	Late spring.
Flowers	Small, white, alone or in clusters.	**Propagation**	Easy to grow from seed in spring, or from a cutting in April.
Flowering season	Summer.		
Fruit	Round, like small cherries, bright red or yellow; they ripen in autumn and last throughout the winter.		

SYNGONIUM

*In Jamaica, if the leaves of the syngonium
wilt because of lack of water or excessive heat, it is
thought to be a bad omen.*

The Latin name, syngonium, comes from the Greek words 'syn', or 'united', and 'gone', or 'womb', to indicate that the two parts of the ovary are joined together. These plants are also known as 'three-fingered', 'five-fingered' or 'goosefoot' plants.

The leaves must be sprayed regularly
The syngonium needs the same kind of care and attention as the scindapsus (see page 92). Be sure to include the underside of the leaves and the stalks when spraying; in this way the plant will absorb enough moisture to maintain its characteristic shiny leaves in good condition.

A light feed of houseplant fertilizer once a week will keep the plant growing well and an occasional spray will be helpful.

The syngonium should be watered every week or so in summer by partially immersing the pot in tepid water for half- to three-quarters of an

The syngonium is an attractive, tolerant plant with no special requirements as regards light and temperature. It makes a perfect houseplant and fits extremely well in both modern and traditional settings.

hour. These plants are most successfully grown in pots with their own in-built water supply, or in water in special containers. Once the plant has reached a certain size, it can be trained up a trellis to create an attractive wall of green.

The most beautiful species
S. auritum, or 'five-fingered plant'.
A climber with bright green leaves.
S. vellozianum
A climber with bronze stems and five-lobed leaves.
S. wendlandii
A climber; the leaves are arrow-shaped when young and three-lobed when mature; bright green in colour.

IDENTIFICATION

Family	Araceae.	**Uses**	As a houseplant.
Genus	Comprises about 15 species.	**Position**	In good light, away from direct sunlight.
Origin	America.	**Soil**	Loam and peat or leafmould with added sand.
Type	Evergreen ornamental plants, often climbers.	**When to plant**	In winter.
Leaves	Arrow-shaped at the tip, with two or four heart-shaped stalks at the base; dark green in colour.	**or re-pot**	
		Propagation	By planting a cutting in sandy soil under glass; roots taken from the parent plant can be grown in water.
Flowers	Inconspicuous; only appear on plants grown in the greenhouse.		

PLANTS WITH COLOURED FOLIAGE

The term 'houseplant' immediately conjures up a picture of green plants such as the ficus or philodendron, palms and ferns. Many beautifully coloured foliage plants can add greatly to the interior decor of any room. For example, the colour combinations of red, yellows and browns of the croton, or the striking purples, reds and whites of the calathea are simply magnificent.

Generally, it is best to use only one or two coloured foliage plants in a group of greenery if you want the plants to look their best. Alternatively, if you have a particularly handsome green foliage plant it could look extremely attractive as contrast in a group of several variegated or coloured foliage plants of the same species. Or you could arrange a few green plants against a background of coloured ones but be sure to leave enough space between each plant so that the light will reach the lower leaves.

Another point to remember is that most coloured foliage plants tend to be more delicate than the green species and their leaves require better light and sometimes more frequent spraying. Since the leaves are often rather delicate it is a good idea to spray the air surrounding them, rather than the leaves themselves. In this way the leaves will absorb all the moisture they need without any risk of being spoiled.

1. *An attractive arrangement of coloured foliage plants.*
2. *The beauty of coloured foliage plants is often highlighted by the contrast of green plants.*

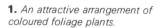

In the following pages we describe a few coloured foliage plants which are easy to grow indoors.

APHELANDRA

In Mexico, the aphelandra is thought to represent passion because of its flame-like flowers and for this reason it is a popular gift between lovers.

The Latin name comes from the Greek and refers to the simple internal structure of the flower. These plants were only introduced to Europe from tropical America during the last century, but they rapidly gained in popularity.

Available species
A.s. 'Brockfeld'
Grown less for its flowers than for its brighter and generally more striking striped foliage.
A.s. leopoldii
Narrower leaves and the yellow flowers here appear through the red bracts held on top of red stems.

A.s. louisae
The variety most frequently seen, popular for its cockscomb of yellow flowers which appear between even brighter yellow bracts.
A. squarrosa
50 cm (20 in) high with lemon yellow or greenish-yellow flowers and more usually seen in the form of its several varieties.

1. Because of its magnificent foliage, the aphelandra is an attractive houseplant even when it is not in flower.
2. The beautiful flowers of the aphelandra.

IDENTIFICATION

Family	Acanthaceae.
Genus	Comprises about 60 species.
Origin	Mexico, Brazil, New Grenada (West Indies).
Type	Small evergreen shrubs or herbaceous clumps, very vigorous.
Leaves	Oval, elongated, sometimes with wavy edges; light green with white or yellow marks; the underside is reddish.
Flowers	Beautiful floral spikes surrounded by bracts, often of a different colour to the flowers. The flowers are orange, yellow or red.
Flowering season	Autumn. The plant can be forced in the greenhouse to flower at other times of the year (winter, summer). The flowers will last some time if the plant is properly looked after.
Uses	As a houseplant.
Position	In the light, away from direct sunlight, draughts and heat sources. In cold climates it can only live in a greenhouse, but in very warm climates it can live outside.
Soil	Use a rich, peaty mixture.
Propagation	This should be done in a greenhouse and left to experts.
Transplanting	This should be done one month after the plant has finished flowering. It can live in the same pot for about one year. When re-potting, use a pot about 2 cm (1 in) larger in diameter than the previous one, and a peaty soil.
Watering	Regular watering is essential. When the plant is not in flower, the leaves benefit by being sprayed occasionally with tepid water.

BEGONIA REX

Some begonias are noted more for their leaves than for their flowers. Here is a fine example.

The begonia is a genus of some 350 species native to all moist tropical countries except Australia. It includes a vast number of easy and popular flowering plants as well as the most vivid and widest ranging collection of those grown for their foliage alone. The *B. rex* varieties have been widely hybridized to produce thousands of varieties of many colour combinations, all of them characterized by the typical lop-sided, heart-shaped leaf. These leaf-interest begonias are all in the rhizomatous group.

Easily grown
Although this group is best known for its interesting foliage pattern and colouration, this does not mean that it produces no flowers, but as a general rule they are of less importance and interest than the striking leaves. The foliage begonias of the *B. rex* group all grow from a rhizome, a spreading underground stem, and all like a light and rich soil that holds moisture well, such as a well rotted leafmould, a loam with plenty of peat or a soil-less compost. The problem with all begonias, not only the foliage types, is that they de-

Matt black and vivid, shining red— examples of the dramatic colourings to be found in the leaves of B. rex.

mand high humidity yet at the same time dislike being too wet at the roots. On the other hand they will accept a wide range of temperatures and will even tolerate a certain amount of indoor darkness, although they grow best in good light.

Many varieties
Plants of the *B. rex* group or type can, in fact, belong to several different species, although they are normally classified together under the one heading. They can be, for example, *B. daedalea*, *B. decora*, *B. imperalis* and several others, all with the characteristic beautifully marked leaves in a range of colours. So many crosses have been made that vast numbers of *B. rex* plants are now circulating with unknown names and unknown parentage, all living under the umbrella christening and varying sometimes less in the leaf shape and colouration than in the flower when this appears. Most have hairy rhizomatous roots, stems and sometimes the undersides of leaves.

IDENTIFICATION

Family	Begoniaceae.
Genus	Some 350 species of flowering and foliage types with vast numbers of cultivars.
Origin	From all moist tropical countries except Australia.
Type	Succulent herbs, sub-shrubs and climbers, the rex varieties usually being in the first group.
Leaves	Alternate, shaped like a lop-sided heart, invariably irregularly toothed.
Flowers	Usually small in this group, of various colours, single.
Flowering season	Dependent on type and season.
Uses	Mainly indoors as a houseplant, sometimes in borders or beds.
Position	In good light but no direct sun.
Soil	An open, free-draining mixture is necessary but one which will hold moisture, such as a soil-less compost.
When to plant	Normally in late winter or early spring.
Propagation	By division of rhizomes.

CALADIUM

The name of this plant means 'fickleness'. In its countries of origin, especially in Guyana, the leaves of the caladium are often used as plates.

The Latin name comes from an ancient Indian word, 'ke-lady'. The exact meaning of this word is not known, but the caladium was first discovered in 1767.

These are difficult plants to grow

The caladium is *not* an easy plant to grow since most of its growing cycle should really take place under greenhouse conditions, but it can be kept attractive for a few weeks in the house.

The pot must be kept in a well lit position, away from direct sunlight. It must be protected from draughts and it should never be moved from its original position. The soil should be watered and the leaves lightly sprayed daily in summer. If the atmosphere is hot and dry the plant may even need watering and spraying twice a day in hot summer weather.

At the end of summer the leaves of the caladium will begin to fade and will eventually drop off. This is the inevitable fate of all plants grown from bulbs since they have a well-defined growing cycle.

The caladium will keep its leaves from February or March right through until October in a greenhouse, but in the house they will only last for up to two months or so. The tubers should be kept dry and replanted in moist peat in the following spring when new growth will quickly appear.

1. *The caladium, with its enormous coloured leaves, is one of our most elegant and decorative houseplants.*
2. *The caladium should be watered carefully to keep the soil moist but not overwatered.*

IDENTIFICATION

Family	Araceae.
Genus	Comprises 16 species with many hybrids.
Origin	Brazil and Guyana.
Type	Herbaceous plants with tuberous roots.
Leaves	Growing directly from the roots on long stems (30 cm or 12 in high); the leaves are up to 60 cm (2 ft) long; the colour varies; on a background of various hues of green, there may be delicate streaks of white, pink, crimson or red, in every kind of pattern.
Flowers	Greenish spathes surrounding a floral spike; not particularly attractive.
Uses	As a houseplant. In very hot and humid climates they can grow outside on the veranda or porch.
Position	In a very well lit place, away from direct sunlight.
Soil	Garden soil mixed with equal parts of peat and leafmould; a handful of sand and a handful of fine charcoal should be added per plant.
When to plant	At the end of the winter.
Propagation	By division of the small tubers which form round the mature ones; division should be carried out in February–March when planting.

CALATHEA

In Brazil, this plant is greatly revered by the indigenous population for its delicate leaves which resemble the plumage of some exotic birds.

The Latin name calathea comes from the Greek 'kalathos', or 'basket', but nobody knows quite why.

These are difficult plants
The calathea is not an easy houseplant to look after. It needs a moist atmosphere and some warmth. Neverthe-less, it is well worth attempting to grow a calathea in the house because they are extremely attractive plants and give great pleasure during their brief life span.

These suggestions on how to care for a calathea should be helpful:

☐ Put the pot in good light but protected from the sun.

☐ Make sure the soil is always kept cool and rather moist but not waterlogged.

☐ Never move the flower pot from its original position and be sure to protect the calathea from the slightest draught.

1. A magnificent example of C. insignis, which makes an excellent houseplant. This tropical plant likes diffused light but must be kept away from direct sunlight and in a temperature not lower than 18°C (65°F).
2. The C. Makoyana has broader leaves than C. insignis, with red streaks on the underside.

IDENTIFICATION

Family	*Marantaceae.*
Genus	*Comprises about 130 species. There are also many varieties and hybrids.*
Origin	*Brazil and Peru.*
Type	*Herbaceous rhizomatous plants which grow up to 1 m (39 in) high in the wild but cultivated plants only reach 50–60 cm (20–24 in) high.*
Leaves	*Very beautiful, coloured green, pink, red, brown and purple in a variety of hues.*

Flowers	*Small, white, insignificant, seldom seen.*
Uses	*As a houseplant; in tropical areas they make splendid garden plants.*
Position	*Diffused light, away from direct sunlight; they need a moist atmosphere and a temperature not lower than 18°C (65°F).*
Soil	*Three parts leaf compost, three parts garden soil, three parts peat, one part sand.*
When to plant or re-pot	*At the end of the summer.*
Propagation	*By division, in the early spring.*

CEROPEGIA

In this country the ceropegia has no special meaning. In Africa, the Philippines and Sri Lanka, the flexible branches of some species, especially the Ceropegia woodii, *are used to weave necklaces for the young brides.*

The Latin name ceropegia comes from the Greek 'keros', 'wax', and 'pege', 'fountain', and describes the strange consistency of the petals and the characteristic shape of the flower. The *Ceropegia woodii* is sometimes known as the 'necklace of hearts' because of its heart-shaped leaves.

The ceropegia, or 'necklace of hearts' is a curious and unusual houseplant. Unfortunately, this attractive little plant is not easy to come by; but with perseverance it should be possible to trace the odd plant or two, and it is extremely easy to increase your stock by taking a cutting.

The species with the most flowers

These are the most popular species:

C. africana
Slender, trailing branches; its leaves are very beautiful, oval and rather succulent; the flowers are green and dark purple.

C. dichotoma
Not a climber; it has flowers of white and lemon yellow.

C. elegans
Bright purple flowers; very suitable for trellises or hanging baskets.

C. sandersonii
Reddish, fleshy branches and large pale green flowers.

C. woodii
Purple branches, grey-green leaves with white markings and pink and white flowers.

IDENTIFICATION

Family	Asclepiadaceae.
Genus	Comprises about 100 species.
Origin	South Africa, southeast Asia, the Philippines, Malabar and the Canaries.
Type	Herbaceous plants or semi-shrubs with long flexible branches, often climbers. They can also be trained to trail their branches. The roots are tuberous. In a European climate they can only grow indoors or in a greenhouse.
Leaves	Fleshy, oval or heart-shaped. Pale green or grey-green, sometimes marked with purple, brown or white.
Flowers	Usually grouped together in clusters and of strange colours varying from pink and brown, green and purple to green and white or bronze and pink.
Flowering season	At various times of the year according to environment. The C. woodii flowers nearly all the time.
Uses	As an ornamental houseplant, particularly suitable for hanging baskets or bamboo trellises.
Position	In a well lit spot, away from direct sunlight.
Soil	Ordinary houseplant compost, mixed with one-third sand.
Watering	Very little. Generally speaking, the ceropegia requires the same treatment as succulent plants (see page 94).
Feeding	Very little. A liquid or powdered fertilizer should be used while plants are growing strongly.
When to plant or re-pot	When the plant is resting and not producing flowers.
Propagation	This is easily done by cutting a branch and planting it in sandy soil or water. It is also easy to divide the tubers.

CHLOROPHYTUM

The chlorophytum means 'you will be young for ever', so the gift of one of these plants is a great compliment. This meaning obviously comes from a characteristic of the chlorophytum which is to put out many long stems with tiny new plants on the end.

The chlorophytum is a graceful houseplant which can be grown outside on mild summer days provided that it is sheltered from the wind and sun. It looks most effective trailing over a parapet or balcony.

The Latin name chlorophytum comes from the Greek 'chloros' or 'green', and 'phyton' or 'plant'. This plant is also known as the 'phalangium', the 'ribbon plant' and the 'spider plant'.

They are easy to look after
The chlorophytum is one of the easiest of all houseplants to look after. It needs water once or twice a week according to season, or it can be grown in a flower pot with its own in-built water supply. Add some soluble fertilizer to the water once a month, according to the directions on the pack. The topsoil should be turned fairly frequently to prevent a crust from forming.

The most beautiful species are:

C. comosum
With leaves 40 cm (16 in) long, dark green. There are several varieties and hybrids with white and green variegated leaves.

C. elatum
The most common houseplant, with leaves 30–40 cm (12–16 in) long and 1 cm ($\frac{1}{2}$ in) wide at the base; pale green. There are varieties with white edges, or with a white strip down the centre of the leaves.

IDENTIFICATION

Family	Liliaceae.
Genus	Comprises about 40 species.
Origin	South Africa and central Asia.
Type	Small perennial herbaceous plants with fibrous, fleshy roots.
Leaves	Evergreen, up to 60 cm (2 ft) long, narrow, ribbon-like, pointed, growing in a thick rosette. In various hues of green but there are many white and green variegated varieties.
Flowers	Tiny, white or green, grouped in terminal clusters.
Flowering season	At different times of year, depending on the environment.
Uses	As a houseplant but it can also be used on an outside balcony.
Position	Good light, but right away from direct sunlight. They do not like the cold or wind.
Soil	Ordinary garden soil mixed with one-third peat and one-third sand.
When to plant	Chlorophytum plants can be temporarily planted out in the garden in summer. Houseplants can be re-potted when the plant has stopped flowering.
Propagation	By removing the tufts of leaves which form at the end of its long stems. These new plants will take root more easily in spring.

CROTON or CODIAEUM

1

2

'You are capricious' is the meaning of this plant's name. With its multi-coloured leaves, the croton is one of the most beautiful of houseplants.

The Latin name codiaeum comes from the Malay name 'kodiho' and it is possible that this itself derives from the Greek word for 'chief', referring to the Malaysian habit of wearing garlands of croton leaves at important religious ceremonies.

The croton genus comprises a large number of species of varying shapes and colours. Many varieties have long, thin leaves but some have arrow-shaped or curled leaves and others have leaves shaped like oak leaves.

The ornamental croton, or coediaeum, is often confused with the croton genus which does not include any ornamental species, only medicinal plants.

A very humid atmosphere
The croton is a most difficult houseplant to keep alive but its wonderful, multi-coloured leaves make it well worth growing for even a few weeks. Here are a few important rules which must be followed:
□ Keep the plant at a constant temperature ranging from 16–20°C (60–70°F).
□ The pot should be in a well

1. Close-up of the variegated foliage of several varieties of croton.
2. A beautiful croton with very variegated leaves. Latest varieties on the market are much more hardy and will tolerate poor home conditions for much longer than earlier types.

lit position, even in direct sunlight except on hot, sunny days. Never move the plant and always protect it from draughts.
□ The soil must always be kept cool, but not water-logged. It is advisable to grow the croton in a flower pot with its own in-built water supply so that it can

absorb the moisture it needs without danger of being overwatered.
□ Spray the air around the leaves every hot and sunny day and every ten days bathe the leaves with cotton wool soaked in tepid water, preferably rainwater. At the same time, lightly disturb the topsoil to prevent a crust from forming.
□ Scale insects sometimes attack the croton, so check the leaves frequently and at the first sign of an attack take immediate remedial action.

IDENTIFICATION

Family	Euphorbiaceae.
Genus	Comprises only about six species, of which only one has been grown in Europe since the last century: the C. variegatum pictum.
Origin	Malaysia and the Moluccas.
Type	Trees with multi-coloured leaves.
Leaves	Evergreen, either lobed or undivided.
Flowers	Inconspicuous.
Uses	As an ornamental houseplant or in a conservatory or garden room; in a very hot climate it can be grown out of doors (in the shade and sheltered from the wind) in a courtyard or patio.
Position	In a well lit position, even in direct sunlight for periods.
Soil	The most suitable is a mixture of one-third garden soil, one-third leafmould, one-sixth peat and one-sixth sand.
When to plant or re-pot	At the end of the winter. This often helps to revive plants which have suffered from a long stay in the house.
Propagation	By taking a cutting—but this must be left to the experts.

DRACAENA and CORDYLINE

1. *An all green variety of* D. fragrans.

2. *A dracaena growing in water.*

'I shall steal your heart': this is the love message of the dracaena, a very popular houseplant. Its flowers are very unexciting and only appear when the plant is grown in a greenhouse or on the Riviera.

The Latin name dracaena comes from the Greek 'drakaina', 'female dragon'. This is possibly because, in the past, the sap of the dracaena was used as the colouring matter which is sometimes known as 'dragon's blood'.

The name cordyline also comes from the Greek 'kordyle', meaning 'club' or 'bludgeon' and evidently referring to the shape of the roots.

IDENTIFICATION

Family	Liliaceae.
Genus	Dracaena comprises about 40 species; Cordyline genus comprises about 20 species.
Origin	Tropical and west Africa, Cape of Good Hope, Indian Ocean Islands, central America.
Type	Herbaceous shrubs or tree-like plants; the latter are composed of a trunk with a tuft of leaves on the top when young, but the trunk thickens and divides up into branches as the plant matures.
Leaves	Oval or elongated and very pointed; the colour varies from bright green to dark green, often with white or yellow stripes or marked with red or purple.
Flowers	Inconspicuous, in large yellowish-green spikes.
Flowering season	Between spring and summer.
Uses	As an ornamental garden plant in a warm climate, or as a houseplant.
Position	In the sun or semi-shade outside; in good light away from direct sunlight indoors.
Soil	Garden soil mixed with one-third peat and one-third sand.
When to plant	In spring; re-potting of indoor plants should be carried out at the end of winter.
Propagation	By layering, in July, using the top of the plant.

Probably the most remarkable member of the dracaena family, which contains about fifty species spread out across the warmer areas of the Old World, is the celebrated *Dracaena draco*.

This is the Dragon Tree of the Canary Islands and it reaches both a great age and a great size.

One famous specimen in Teneriffe—destroyed by a hurricane in 1868—reached a height of 24 m (79 ft) and was rumoured to be 6000 years old.

These rules must be carefully followed

The dracaena and the cordyline need the same care. When grown outside in a warm climate they need no special care so long as they are protected in winter against winds blowing off the sea.

So far as indoor plants are concerned, these points must be remembered:

☐ They do *not* like direct sunlight, draughts, being moved about too much, overwatered roots, too much water on their leaves; drops of water will mark the leaves and turn them yellow.
☐ They need a lot of light and a constant temperature, not too hot.
☐ Regular watering according to the size of the plant.
☐ To be fed every two weeks or so with a liquid or soluble balanced fertilizer.
☐ Well drained soil and repotting every two years, at the most, into a slightly larger container using a mixture of garden soil, one-third peat and one-third sand.

The most attractive species of dracaena are:

D. fragrans
Out of doors this plant quickly grows into a tree, but it is usually used as a houseplant. Its bright green leaves have yellow or ivory stripes, especially the *lindenii* and *massangeana* varieties.

D. godseffiana
Its bright green leaves are covered with white or ivory streaks.

1. *Splendid example of* D. fragrans lindenii *which is one of the most attractive and easy houseplants.*

2. *A recent* D. deremensis *hybrid with very pretty leaves.*

*The name dracaena is
frequently given to both the dracaena
and the cordyline genus.*

D. goldieana
Not very large with beautiful silver markings, pink when young.

D. hookeriana
Even when grown out of doors this species is not more than 2 m (6 ft) high. Its leaves are often edged with white; the *latifolia* and *variegata* varieties have pretty variegated leaves.

D. marmorata
Sword-shaped leaves of bright green with white marks. This species is not so well known nor as easy to obtain as it deserves to be.

D. sanderiana
Bright green leaves with white stripes; a very popular houseplant.

The most attractive cordyline species are:

C. stricta
1–2 m (3–6 ft) high with dark serrated leaves.

C. terminalis
A small species with fairly broad leaves. It is mostly used as an ornamental houseplant because of its beautiful bronze and red or pink and white variegated leaves. Many varieties.

The 'plant of happiness'
In recent years in some countries a houseplant known, among other names, as the 'plant of happiness' has come into fashion. This is a dracaena grown with a special technique. A cutting is taken from a section of the dracaena trunk that has no leaves on it. The cutting is then put in water to form its roots. New shoots soon begin to sprout out of the sides of the trunk and this creates a most unusual and attractive effect.

1. *The cordyline is very like the dracaena and it requires the same care and attention.*
2. C. terminalis, *known popularly as 'flaming dragon tree', is one of the most beautiful houseplants because of its red and bronze leaves.*

86

FITTONIA

This has no special meaning in flower language, but certain tribes in the Para of Brazil believe the fittonia is a magic plant that contains messages hidden in the vein patterns of its leaves which can only be read by the village soothsayer.

The Latin names comes from Sarah and Elizabeth Fitton, joint authors of 'Botanical Conversations'. These sisters were great friends of the well-known English naturalist, Robert Brown. The fittonia is also known as the 'hieroglyphic plant'.

The fittonia does not need special attention
It is not complicated to grow but it does need careful and regular watering. As a general rule it should be watered in summer once or twice a week, preferably by partially immersing the pot in a basin of water for two hours. The leaves are rather delicate. Feed the plant every two weeks with compound houseplant fertilizer.

Keep your fittonia in a well lit position away from direct sunlight.

The most attractive species
The fittonia does not need as much light as many other houseplants and it is therefore particularly suitable for a poorly lit corner. Here are the most attractive species:

F. argyroneura
A prostrate-growing plant with trailing branches; its leaves are 10 cm (4 in) long, bright green with pale silvery veins.

The fittonia is one of the most delicate and attractive houseplants. It has beautiful leaves and flowers and is difficult to keep in good condition for long without warm and humid conditions.

F. gigantea
A small upright shrub 50 cm (20 in) high; the leaves have crimson veins and this species has pretty pink flowers.

F. vershaffeltii
Dark green leaves with bright red veins.

IDENTIFICATION

Family	Acanthaceae.
Genus	Comprises three species.
Origin	Brazil and Peru.
Type	Herbaceous upright or prostrate growing plants.
Leaves	Evergreen, oval, rounded, often velvety; the colour varies from bright green with red or white veins, to yellowish-green with white or yellow veins. The veins are very conspicuous.
Flowers	Inconspicuous, growing in a spike.
Uses	As an ornamental houseplant.
Position	In a well lit spot away from direct sunlight; they can also survive in poorly lit places.
Soil	Ordinary peaty compost for houseplants.
When to plant or re-pot	Autumn.
Propagation	By cutting off the end of a stem below the two uppermost leaves and shoot and burying it about 2 cm (1 in) in moist sandy soil. If this is done in a warm atmosphere the roots will form in about ten days. The new plant should then be potted in a small pot (6 cm or 2½ in in diameter) using houseplant compost, mixed with one-third sand. When the roots have filled the pot, the plant should be transplanted into its proper container (about 10–12 cm or 4–5 in in diameter).

MARANTA

'You are bold and beautiful' is the hidden message of this exotic plant. In its native tropical America religious dancers decorate themselves with the wreaths of orchids and maranta leaves. If a young man gives his lover a maranta leaf, this is tantamount to breaking off his relationship with her publicly because she has been unfaithful.

The Latin name maranta comes from the 16th-century Venetian botanist and naturalist, Bartolomeo Maranti. This plant has several strange names in various parts of the world: 'Arrowroot' in Bermuda, 'Yuquilla' in South America and 'Hoang Tinh' in Indo China.

It does not like to be moved
The maranta has to be looked after in much the same way as most other ornamental houseplants, especially the calathea (see page 80), but it does need a very light and open soil mixture such as is obtained by mixing four parts loam with one part leaf-mould and one part sand.

The maranta requires a great deal of water from the spring until autumn and much less in the winter to give the rhizomes a long rest. The pot should be kept in a well lit position, away from direct sunlight and protected from draughts. It should not be moved too frequently.

The most beautiful species are:
M. bicolor
Elliptic or linear leaves, 30 cm (12 in) long, bright green with a symmetrical purple design on each side of the central vein.

M. leuconeura
Stems 30 cm (12 in) long and leaves 15 cm (6 in) wide, grey-green with dark green, white or purple markings. The species is less striking than its two popular varieties:

M.l. kerchoveana
Darker patches on the green leaves, and

M.l. massangeana
Beautifully marked and patterned leaves in green, gold and red.

M. ruiziana
Leaves with very pronounced markings along the edges in varying hues of green. This species is not as well known as it deserves to be.

The maranta is one of the most beautiful ornamental houseplants; it likes plenty of light and well fertilized, sharply drained soil, which will retain just the right amount of moisture for its needs. The maranta also needs feeding at fairly frequent intervals. The picture shows a M. leuconeura, probably the most attractive species.

IDENTIFICATION

Family	Marantaceae.	*Flowers*	Insignificant, white in a raceme.
Genus	Comprises about 15 species.	*Uses*	As a houseplant; in its native tropical
Origin	Tropical America.		America the rhizomes of the M. arundinacea
Type	Herbaceous, upright or prostrate plants with		are used to make arrowroot.
	rhizomatous roots.	*Position*	In a good light, away from direct sunlight,
Leaves	Shaped like a scabbard at the base of the		in a warm spot.
	leaf, held on stems of varying lengths. They	*Soil*	Soft and well fertilized.
	are oval and rounded at the tip, bright	*When to plant*	End of the autumn or in spring.
	green with markings of darker green,	*or re-pot*	
	purple or brown.	*Propagation*	By dividing the rhizomes in spring.

NIDULARIUM

As far as we know this plant has no special meaning. Its only peculiarity is that when it grows wild, snakes and birds drink from the water which is held by the leaves at the plant's centre.

The Latin name nidularium comes from the Latin word 'nidus' or 'nest', referring to the depression formed by the leaves of this plant. The nidularium was first heard of half way through the last century.

How to look after it
The nidularium does not like a dry or overheated atmosphere. Keep the central depression filled with water as with most other bromeliads. The only time the soil should be moistened is when you feed the plant once a month. Spray the leaves every five or six days with rainwater (or other soft water) until the flowers appear.

The most attractive species are:
N. carolinae tricolor
(Correctly, *Neoregelia carolinae tricolor*)
The best known, most frequently seen and most spectacular variety; large, with green, pink and yellow leaves

and a vivid red centre when the little flowers appear.
N. fulgens
Made up of about 30 leaves; produces insignificant violet flowers and the central leaves turn bright red.
N. innocentii
White flowers also produced when the centre turns bright scarlet, and thickly grouped leaves with spiny edges. The central leaves are reddish-purple.
N. procerum
Blue flowers and very spiny leaves which turn purple at the centre.
N. purpureum
Red flowers and leaves with red and bronze shading at the centre.
N. rutilans
Vermilion flowers and the centre of the plant is red and pink. This is one of the most spectacular species.
N. striatum
Very like the *N. innocentii* but the leaves have bright green and white longitudinal stripes.

The nidularium is a very beautiful houseplant, with its characteristic red centre in the middle of a thick clump of leaves. The flowers appear in the centre of the plant and can be white or blue. The N. tricolor (picture 1) is a recent hybrid of the N. innocenti species (picture 2) and is probably more correctly known as Neoregelia carolinae tricolor.

IDENTIFICATION

Family	Bromeliaceae.
Genus	Comprises about 30 species.
Origin	Brazil.
Type	Ornamental hothouse plants.
Leaves	They grow in a rosette; they are very long with serrated edges, thick, almost succulent, dark green and shiny. The central leaves are shorter than the outer ones and turn a variety of hues of bright red when the flowers appear.
Flowers	Growing in an attractive inflorescence, they can be white, violet or blue, but are mainly insignificant.
Flowering season	At various times of year depending on the environment, but usually in winter.
Uses	As a houseplant or hothouse plant.
Position	In the light away from direct sunlight.
Soil	A mixture of garden soil, one-third peat and one-third leaf compost and sand.
When to plant or re-pot	As soon as the plant stops flowering, usually at the end of winter.
Propagation	By taking off the new shoots which form at the side of the parent plant.

PEPEROMIA

This plant's sap has medicinal properties. In the Pacific islands it is used to cure skin and eye infections.

The Latin name peperomia comes from the Greek 'peperi' or 'pepper', and 'omorios' or 'like', which refers to its similarity to the 'piper' genus to which the pepper plant belongs.

Be careful when watering

Unlike most houseplants, the peperomia does not need much water because it is a fairly succulent plant (that is, it retains a great deal of water) and it does not like a very humid atmosphere. The best way to water the peperomia is by immersing the pot in water for about an hour once every ten days or

at longer intervals if the soil still feels moist.

Lightly loosen the topsoil once or twice a season to allow air to the roots. It is not advisable to spray the leaves.

During the summer months the peperomia can be kept outside provided that it is in absolute shade and sheltered from the rain.

The most attractive species are
P. caperata
Thick clumps of leaves on short stems 10 cm (4 in) long; the leaves are dark green and velvety with parallel furrows. The *tricolor* variety is

1. *The peperomia is a beautiful houseplant with very attractive foliage. The picture shows* P. caperata *with its deeply furrowed, green leaves and 'rat's tail' flowers.*
2. *A magnificent variety,* P. sandersii *with its silver and green variegated leaves.*

very beautiful with ivory leaves and deep green markings.
P. hederaefolia
Small, with metallic grey-green, lightly ridged leaves.
P. maculosa
Spear-shaped oval leaves of bright green with purple stalks.
P. magnoliaefolia
The best known species, with

glossy green and gold fleshy leaves.
P. marmorata
Lanceolate or pointed leaves of deep green with white markings.
P. metallica
30 cm (12 in) high with oblong lanceolate leaves, dark green with metallic reflections and pale stripes. The stalks are red or violet.
P. sandersii
15 cm (6 in) high with oval, silver and green leaves and bright green veins.
P. scaneleus
Similar to *P. magnoliaefolia*, but with smaller leaves and a trailing habit.

IDENTIFICATION

Family	Piperaceae.	**Uses**	As a houseplant.
Genus	Comprises about 400 species.	**Position**	In good light, away from direct sunlight.
Origin	America and other tropical and sub-tropical areas of the Pacific.	**Soil**	Peaty mixture or garden soil mixed with one-third peat and one-third sand.
Type	Annual or perennial herbaceous plants.	**When to plant**	In autumn or at the end of winter.
Leaves	Undivided, fleshy, striped or marked, with veins or dots, in various shades of green with reddish or silvery lights.	**or re-pot**	
		Propagation	By taking a cutting in spring of a leaf and section of stem and planting it in very sandy soil, which should be kept cool but not moist. The pot should be placed in a well lit spot, away from direct sunlight.
Flowers	Inconspicuous, in a white or cream floral spike.		

PILEA

The meaning of this plant is 'you have wounded me.' It probably stems from a characteristic of one species of the plant: when the pollen is ripe, this pilea throws up little clouds. The filaments holding the pollen spring up to release the pollen in a burst. The flower buds open at rapid intervals, like miniature machine guns in fire.

The pilea is one of the most popular houseplants because of its attractive silver and green leaves which contrast beautifully with the green foliage houseplants.

The name pilea comes from the Latin 'pileus' or 'hat', in reference to the felt beret which ancient Romans wore on feast days. An internal part of the flower is said to look like one of these berets. The *Pilea muscosa* is also known as the 'artillery plant' and the 'firework plant' because of the strange way in which its pollen is disseminated.

IDENTIFICATION

Family	Urticaceae.
Genus	Comprises about 200 species.
Origin	Tropical regions except for Australia.
Type	Herbaceous annuals or perennials.
Leaves	Alternate, undivided or indented, oval, with pronounced veins, often with silver or bronze streaks.
Flowers	Inconspicuous.
Uses	As a houseplant or in a garden (P. muscosa).
Position	In good light, away from direct sunlight; in semi-shade outside.
Soil	Garden soil mixed with one-quarter peat and one-quarter sand.
When to plant	Outside and indoors at the end of winter.
Propagation	By taking a cutting in April or by sowing seed in the greenhouse in March.

Not too much humidity

The pilea requires much the same treatment as most other houseplants: plenty of light, not too much heat and no draughts. The soil should be kept cool but not water-logged because this plant absorbs water with ease. If the water is unable to drain away from the somewhat succulent stems, they may begin to rot and the plant will lose its leaves.

Feed the plant every two weeks.

When the pilea grows too straggly, take out the growing tips. The plant will then form new shoots at the base and this will improve its shape. Pilea plants grown out of doors require the same attention as those grown indoors.

The most attractive species are:

P. cadierei (Aluminium plant)
About 30 cm (12 in) high, with bright green leaves spotted in a shiny silver patina. This is an attractive and popular houseplant.

P. muscosa
Known as artillery plant or pistol plant, an annual which can also be grown outside; 15 cm (6 in) high and flowers in summer.

P. nummularifolia
A prostrate-growing perennial with rounded leaves; very beautiful.

P. spruceana
Very small with rough dark green and bronze leaves. This species is also very beautiful.

SCINDAPSUS or POTHOS

*There is no
special meaning
in flower
language for this
plant. In the
Pacific islands,
the long tendrils
of the pothos
are used to
make crowns
for widows
attending wedding
ceremonies.*

The plant we know as scindapsus is called pothos by the Americans and some Europeans. Each is a different genus but both belong to the family araceae. It is also known as 'wandering sailor'.

Scindapsus is an ancient Greek name for a plant-like ivy. The Latin name pothos comes from 'potha', the name given to an unidentified species of this genus in Sri Lanka.

This plant, which grows wild in a tropical climate, makes an excellent houseplant as it is so easy to grow.

It can be successfully grown in water
The scindapsus really thrives in water since it can then absorb all the moisture it needs without difficulty. The technique is very simple. A

1. *The scindapsus or pothos, one of the most attractive and easy houseplants to grow, lives very happily in water in a suitable glass container. This particular technique ensures that the plant will absorb all the moisture it needs without any risk of the roots rotting.*
2. *The long tendrils of the scindapsus can either be staked or trained up a trellis, or else left to trail freely.*

plant that has already been growing in soil can be adapted to grow in water. Alternatively, a cutting can be put in water to take root (which occurs rapidly), then put in a suitable glass container where it can continue to grow in water.

The scindapsus is also easy to grow in compost and it should be looked after in

much the same way as the philodendron (see page 68). It is important to take care when watering because, like the philodendron, the scindapsus does not like stale water around its roots.

The most beautiful species Scindapsus aureus
Is the only species that is grown as a houseplant. It is similar to *Philodendron scandens* in shape and size but has a more marbled colouring. There is, in fact, a species of pothos which is known as *P. scandens*. There are one or two varieties of *S. aureus* which have become popular, particularly one called 'marble queen' with a greater variegation than normal in its leaf colour.

IDENTIFICATION

Family	Araceae.	**Uses**	As a houseplant.
Genus	Comprises about 20 species.	**Position**	In good light away from direct sunlight.
Origin	Asia, Australia, Pacific Islands, Madagascar.	**Soil**	Peat mixed with one-third leafmould and a little sand.
Type	Climbers with long tendrils, sometimes woody.	**When to plant or re-pot**	At the end of autumn or at the end of winter, when the plant is resting.
Leaves	Heart-shaped, thick, shiny, bright green with white or gold markings.	**Propagation**	By taking a cutting in April and planting it in very sandy soil in the greenhouse, under a cloche, or in water.
Flowers	Small and inconspicuous; houseplants seldom flower.		

VRIESIA

*'The power of love'
is the meaning of this plant;
no doubt due to its
habit of clinging
to trees and rocks in a way
which seems to defy
the laws of nature.
Like all epiphytic plants
the vriesia has
a certain magical quality
and a strong will to survive.*

The vriesia is a houseplant which needs a great deal of light away from direct sunlight. It should not be watered too frequently, but the central 'vase' should always be kept full.

The Latin name vriesia comes from the Dutch botanist, W. H. de Vriese, who lived from 1806–62. We do not know of any colloquial names for this plant, which is sometimes confused with the tillandsia, or 'daughter of the air'.

It does not like too much humidity
The vriesia is fairly easy to look after, even in the house. In a hot climate it can live outside during the fine weather if it is in a well protected position in the shade.

It must not be watered too often: just keep the central cup or vase filled at all times. The leaves benefit from frequent spraying in summer. Feed the plant once a month with a powdered or liquid fertilizer, pouring this on the soil rather than into the cup.

When the flowers begin to fade, cut off the long stem at the base immediately so that the plant will not waste its strength. When it has flowered, the plant itself may begin to fade and eventually die, leaving two or more new shoots at the base which should be carefully removed and planted in very sandy soil to take root.

When the new plants have formed a good tuft of roots, they can be transplanted into slightly larger containers. After one or two years the new plants may even flower but, in any case, the leaves will provide an attractive ornament, particularly well-suited to a modern setting.

The most attractive species
Although there are a number of species of vriesia (and indeed of all other bromeliads), few are to be found outside botanical collections. As a general rule, only one species of vriesia is frequently seen and easy to obtain and this is *V. splendens*, with chocolate or purple horizontal bands across the large leaves and a dramatic flower spike sometimes nearly 60 cm (2 ft) long which terminates with a 'flaming sword' of long lasting scarlet bracts.

V. fenestralis
Less dramatic, greenish-yellow flowers, but its leaves are strikingly marked with fine and delicate lines.
V. hieroglyphica
Attractive not for its dull yellow flowers but for the markings on the leaves, similar to hieroglyphics.
V. tessellata
Somewhat more interesting yellow flowers but is grown more for its distinctively marked leaves, mainly green and yellow. There are a number of varieties with leaves marked in pink, in white and yellow and with a marbled appearance.

Family	Bromeliaceae.
Genus	Comprises about 100 species.
Origin	Central America.
Type	Perennial plants often epiphytic.
Leaves	Growing in a central rosette, elongated, fleshy, green, striped or mottled.
Flowers	Often accompanied by attractively coloured bracts; they grow in a spike, often forked, in yellow or red.
Flowering season	In summer, but grown in a greenhouse they can flower at other times of year, even in winter.
Uses	As an ornamental houseplant.
Position	In good light away from direct sunlight.
Soil	One-third ordinary soil, one-third peat, one-third sand and leafmould.
When to plant or re-pot	After the plant has flowered and when it is resting.
Propagation	By cutting away the new shoots which form at the base of the plant.

1–2–3. *Cacti and succulents are popular largely because of their striking appearance and easy cultivation. Provided that they are grown in the right type of soil and watered correctly, they can survive for many years. They look very effective in a shallow terracotta bowl (1–3). In summer they can be taken outside, so long as they are not allowed to become waterlogged during periods of summer rain.*

The term 'succulent' describes the fleshy nature of the plant tissues. This group of plants includes a large variety of houseplants belonging to many different families but with one characteristic in common: they are all 'xerophytic'. In other words, they are specially adapted to life in a hot, dry atmosphere with plenty of light. As a result of their special 'spongy' structure they are able to retain large quantities of water and to limit their breathing. The leaves of succulent plants have an extremely small surface area and some plants only have stems with no leaves at all.

Soil mixture
Succulent plants must have a particular mixture of soil. If the mixture has all the necessary ingredients and the correct degree of permeability, the plants will grow satisfactorily and watering will present no particular problems. The best composition is:
☐ One-third well sieved peat.
☐ One-third garden soil.
☐ One-third well washed river sand.
☐ A small teaspoonful of powdered chalk.

☐ A little powdered vegetable charcoal can be added to the chalk to prevent fermentation or mould.

Spread a layer of gravel and charcoal lumps on the base of the pot and around the plant to facilitate drainage.

In a very hot climate (especially when cacti are grown in the ground) place some peat round the plant from June to September. This will slow down evaporation and help to keep the plant in good condition. Do not overwater since this can cause permanent damage, even if the plant does show dramatic signs of revival at first.

Be careful when watering
It is essential to give succulent plants the correct amount of water. Overwatering is particularly damaging: the leaves and stalks turn soft and transparent and they 'bleed' at the slightest touch. If rot attacks the base of the plant where it joins the root, the plant will droop and may eventually die. To avoid this danger the following rules should be carefully followed:

Temperature
The water must never be too cold: always at room temperature.

The short-lived blooms of succulent plants are among the most brilliant of all flowers.

Frequency

In winter, most succulent houseplants (in a hot atmosphere) should be watered no more than once a fortnight. Plants grown in an unheated greenhouse or veranda, where the temperature does not rise above 12°C (55°F), should be watered once a month. Most cacti (as apart from other succulents) should not be watered at all in winter. From May to November watering should be increased gradually when changing from a winter to a summer pattern of watering (and vice versa).

Quantity

This varies according to the size and type of plant and the prevailing temperature. If you do not wish to run the risk of over- or underwatering, the pot can be partially immersed in a basin of water for not more than an hour. It is important for the moisture to penetrate right through the pot, without making it waterlogged. Do this only in spring or summer.

Spraying

The main stem can be sprayed once a week in warm periods.

Carefully controlled feeding

These plants require carefully controlled feeding. Mix a little powdered manure with the soil when planting, according to the instructions on the pack.

During the growing period feed the plant once a month with a soluble fertilizer (only half the prescribed dose). This will help the formation of new shoots and flower buds and will also keep the plant in good condition.

How to protect them

Check all succulent plants frequently for any sign of pests or disease. Their commonest enemies are *Botrytis cinerea* and *Phytophthora cactorum*. These fungi attacks occur most often when the plants are overwatered. The best preventive action, apart from taking great care when watering, is to treat the plants once a month with a fungicide.

Mealy bugs, aphids, red spiders, thrips and slugs also attack succulent plants and can be cleared with a proprietory insecticide used according to instructions.

When to re-pot

Re-potting should usually be done every year while the plant is resting (or when it is not forming new shoots or flowering). This is usually at the end of autumn and throughout the winter. Houseplants often vary from this norm, so the best time to re-pot these succulents is as soon as they finish flowering. Do not use very large pots, 2–3 cm (1–1½ in) in diameter bigger than the previous pot will be quite sufficient. Tiny plants in pots of 2–3 cm (1–1½ in) diameter are an exception to this rule. When they outgrow their pots they will need something considerably larger.

How to increase your stock

The propagation of succulent plants is not difficult and is usually done by taking a cutting of a leaf or branch and planting it to form roots. The cutting should be left to dry in the shade for a few days to allow the sap from the wound to congeal.

The cutting should then be planted in a pot with very sandy soil or in dry peat, in the shade, sheltered from the wind. While the cutting is forming its roots spray it

An aloe grown as a houseplant. With a little water and plenty of light, these plants will produce beautiful flowers.

with water every other day.

The lower end of the cutting can be dusted with special hormone rooting powder or liquid to help it to take root more quickly.

The best known succulent plants

The most popular succulent plants grouped under their family headings are:

Cactaceae

Cephalocereus

An erect plant that has many species and varieties, all with very stiff, short spines and long, flexible white thorns which sometimes look like a tuft of hair. The flowers are white, violet, pink or red. *C. senilis* is sometimes called 'old man's cactus'.

Cereus

Has a ribbed cylindrical stem covered in spines with numerous lateral branches. There are many species and varieties with lovely nocturnal flowers which are nearly always white.

Echinocactus

A small barrel-shaped plant with a ribbed stem covered in very many strong spines. It produces flowers of differing shapes and sizes in a variety of colours, mainly yellows.

Echinopsis

A ribbed spherical spiny stem. It produces beautiful white, pink or purple flowers, often scented, in summer.

Epiphyllum

It has long, segmented fleshy leaves with no spines and flowers copiously in the spring with white, pink, scarlet or purple blooms which last only a day or two but appear in frequent succession.

Mammillaria

Comprises numerous species and varieties which are

1

3

2

4

mainly cylindrical or spherical in shape with regular tubercles growing spirally up the main stem; its flowers can be yellow, purple, pink or white.

Notocactus
Elongated globular stems, divided into ribs or tubercles and mainly yellow flowers.

1–2–3–4–5. *Succulent plants are very attractive and their short-lived flowers are brilliantly coloured and often scented. This page shows the flowers of the*
1. Cereus jamacaru
2. Chamaecereus silvestrii
3. Sempervivum montanum
4. Rebutia
and a mammillaria *(5) on the opposite page.*

Opuntia
Some of these prickly pears have spatula-shaped leaves and others a cylindrical stem with many branches; they are sometimes covered in hard spines of varying lengths; the flowers are red or yellow and the fruit is often edible.

Selenicereus
Long, cylindrical, flexible stems with spines frequently woolly. It usually flowers at night, with white blooms so magnificent that plants are known as 'queen of the night'.

Trichocereus
These plants branch out at the base and have very developed spines; the white flowers usually come out at night.

6–7. *Cacti and succulent plants can be attractively arranged about the house. Picture 6 shows a beautiful display of flowering chamaecereus, and in picture 7 there are several flowering cacti growing in a bowl.*

6

7

Zygocactus
Very like the epiphyllum, with strange segmented stems. It produces beautiful scarlet or white flowers with purple fruit. The best known species is the *Z. truncatus,* usually called Christmas cactus.

5

Crassulaceae
Cotyledon
Comprises several species and varieties with fleshy leaves and branches. The flowers grow in a spike and can be red, white, yellow or green.
Crassula
An erect shrubby plant for low growing. Flowers can be red, white, pink or yellow.
Echeveria
The leaves usually grow in a central rosette and the flowers are generally red, but can also be yellow, orange or pink.
Kalanchoe
See page 35.
Sedum
This comprises many species with very fleshy leaves which sometimes grow in clusters. The flowers can be yellow, white, pink, purple, red or green.

Euphorbiaceae
Euphorbia caput-medusae
Cylindrical trailing branches surround the central stem. It produces small, solitary but very pretty flowers.
Euphorbia fulgens
Also known as the 'plant of love'; it has horizontal branches with long, slender leaves of bright green. The yellow flowers are unexciting, but they are surrounded by attractive scarlet bracts.

Euphorbia splendens (E. millii)
Also known as 'crown of thorns'. It has branches covered with cruel spines and terminal clusters of bright green oval leaves. The vivid scarlet flowers are produced almost all the year round. There is also a yellow-flowered variety.

Liliaceae
Aloe (see page 95)
Gasteria
Very like the aloe. It has fleshy mottled spineless leaves growing in a central rosette. The pink or red flowers are streaked with green and are tubular in shape and wider at the base.

Asclepiadaceae
Ceropegia
See page 81.
Composite
Kleinia
With fleshy, cylindrical, joined stems and small clusters of flowers.

The term 'houseplant' normally refers to the usual plants from many parts of the world, frequently exotic and tropical, which rely mainly on their longevity in the home and the beauty of their shape and foliage for their popularity.

For example, the ficus is not a particularly attractive plant in itself (it is not even as pretty as a common wild fern), but when it grows 1m (39 in) or more in height and branches out into an interesting formation, it can be an impressive sight.

Several special techniques or treatments can be applied to growing houseplants and these produce extremely attractive and unusual results. Many of these techniques can only be used for small or even miniature plants.

Hydroponics (see page 102)
Plants everywhere: plants in bottles, plants underwater and now ... amphibious plants. There are special glass vases made in dark shades of glass for growing plants in water, suspended on a special grid so that the roots can trail in the water.

Bottle gardens (see page 105)
These almost always use small plants. A carboy or demijohn will make an excellent 'lilliput' greenhouse with the same mysterious atmosphere as an aquarium. Here, ferns, selaginella or adiantum can all live together in ideal conditions to provide a beautiful and exotic decoration for the living room.

Bonsai (see page 108)
Bonsai is a very unusual technique. It is the Japanese art of dwarfing plants, which can be applied to any genus. Trees which would normally grow up to 20–30 m (60–100 ft) are reduced to a mere 80–90 cm (30–35 in) in height. By this method oak trees hundreds of years old will only grow to 1 m (39 in) tall; tiny apple trees are covered with blossom and fruit every year. Cypress trees more than a century old can be carried about on a tea-tray. This is a real miracle of patience, a quality for which orientals are renowned. Bonsai is rapidly gaining in popularity throughout Europe.

Cut flowers (see page 119)
When considering houseplants we must not forget the immense decorative value of cut flowers, which really come into a category all of their own. Although, theoretically, cut flowers should appeal to keen gardeners in spring and summer when they grow in the garden or on the balcony, it is in winter that they really come into their own.

1. *Cut flowers provide a much-appreciated decorative element in the house, especially if the shapes of the individual flowers are shown off to their best advantage.*
2. *A fine specimen of a philodendron Like the one shown on Page 68, this is also grown in water.*

First a month-by-month guide to plant care and indoor gardening.

1. Keep the plants off the floor to avoid damage if you have underfloor heating.
2. An attractive bottle garden made out of a huge glass ball. You must use plants which like the same conditions and care for this type of arrangement.

Gardening is without a doubt one of the simplest and most accessible of all pastimes. It is also relaxing and is both physically and psychologically satisfying. This opinion is held by many sociologists who are currently fighting to ensure that in the future everyone will have access to a balcony or terrace where he can at the very least enjoy his own miniature hanging garden. If this is not possible, an attractive garden can be created within the walls of the house itself.

Houseplants are not all easy to grow since many of them originate from tropical or subtropical areas where they are used to a constant temperature of 16–20°C (60–70°F), plenty of diffused light away from direct sunlight and a humid atmosphere. In the woods and jungles where the ficus, philodendron, croton and dracaena grow wild, the problem of light does not exist because the sun's rays filter through the trees to provide a perfect habitat for the vegetation below.

The intense heat in the jungle creates the right degree of humidity in the air. This vapour condenses on the leaves during the night and returns to earth as droplets of water. These conditions can be more or less reproduced in the greenhouse where many exotic houseplants are grown. These require very open fertile soil which can retain a considerable quantity of moisture, diffused light and a humid atmosphere.

These hothouse conditions should be recreated in the house on a reduced scale if houseplants are to be grown successfully:

☐ Keep the pots away from direct sunlight.

☐ Protect plants from cold draughts.

☐ Water the plants with extreme care and make sure that the soil does not become waterlogged.

☐ Spray the foliage occasionally in warm weather to keep the atmosphere humid.

The plants must not be moved about too often because each time a plant is moved it wastes valuable energy when trying to angle itself correctly towards the light.

These precautions alone will not keep your houseplants in good condition. A precise calendar of plant care should be scrupulously followed, like the one given on the following pages.

JANUARY

Make sure the leaves are clean

This is a difficult time for houseplants because they have been shut up in a hot, dry, possibly rather airless atmosphere for a long time. It is essential to clean both the upper and underside of the leaves, using a piece of cotton wool soaked in tepid water. Hairy-leaved species should only be cleaned with a dry piece of cotton wool.

Remember

to remove any brown, brittle or yellow leaves and try to find out the cause. Yellowing leaves are often the result of overwatering or a deficiency of iron or some other nutritive substance.

Take special care of winter-flowering species to ensure that their soil is always kept cool and that they do not lose their flowers prematurely. Check pot holders to make sure they do not contain any stagnant water which could drown the lower roots.

Lift and store bulbs of plants which have flowered at Christmas and the New Year. They should be lifted as soon as the flowers have died and put in a box of sandy soil. Water this slightly and place it in a cool, shaded place or even outside under a covering of wood shavings and a plastic sheet.

FEBRUARY

Continue with the January routine

Plants which were suffering from excessive heat and a dry atmosphere in January will need even more care by February, so continue with the January routine, spraying the leaves even more frequently if this appears necessary.

Be very careful with forced flowering plants (cyclamen, primula, cineraria and azalea). The best results are often achieved by keeping these plants in the coolest room in the house, in good light, when they are first purchased, and only moving them to their permanent position when they are thoroughly acclimatized to their new surroundings.

Remember

to avoid putting plants in direct sunlight since this can badly damage the leaves, especially if they are wet. Do *not* put your plants outside too early even if the weather is warmer. It is always better to be safe than sorry and to wait until the warmer weather has quite definitely arrived before putting them out.

Cut euphorbia plants (poinsettias) right back (leaving only a few centimetres showing above the earth) when the bracts have fallen off. In May these plants can be re-potted and put outside to start growing again.

MARCH

Fresh air for the plants

Houseplants have now been living in an overheated airless atmosphere with insufficient humidity and oxygen for three or four months. If it is warm enough outside, open the windows wide to let in fresh air and moisture. This will help to reactivate the flow of sap and start the plants growing again.

Remember

to spray both the upper and underside of the leaves occasionally. Lightly loosen the topsoil to break up the crusty surface. Water the plants a little more frequently with smaller quantities than usual to keep the soil very cool and to ensure that the plants are never thirsty since this could be particularly damaging at this time of year.

Begin feeding the plants with small doses of balanced fertilizer. Spray the leaves of large leaved plants with a good leaf polish so that they can absorb atmospheric moisture more effectively. Protect the plants from direct contact with the air outside until the outdoor temperature has reached 16–18°C (60–65°F).

APRIL

Be careful of draughts

This is the most active phase in the houseplant's growing cycle, so special care is needed at this time. In the first instance begin to feed the plants more freely. Now that the windows are often open it is important to protect houseplants from cold draughts. Be particularly careful of direct sunlight since this could scorch the leaves, especially if they are wet.

Rainwater is very valuable for houseplants and as the April rainfall is usually high, it is a good idea to collect as much of it as possible to store indoors for use during the warmer months.

Remember

to loosen the topsoil gently and fairly frequently to prevent a hard crust from forming. This will allow water and many nutritive substances to pass through and be absorbed more quickly by the plant. Add some fresh compost to each pot.

Spray the leaves occasionally with tepid water. Pinch out the growing tips of any plants which have lost their leaves on the lower half of the trunk. This is particularly advisable for the scindapsus and philodendron.

Check pot holders regularly to make sure they have not collected any stale water as this could seriously damage the roots.

Intensify the feeding programme to help encourage new growth at this

crucial time in the plant's life cycle.

Move succulent plants closer to the window. During the winter these plants tend to become rather 'leggy' through lack of light.

And *never* use cold water on your plants.

MAY

A beauty treatment

Clean each leaf separately (excluding hairy or velvety plants) with cotton wool soaked in tepid water. This should be carefully wiped over the upper and underside of each leaf to keep it green and shining.

When the foliage is dry, spray the plant with water and a proprietary foliar feed. Make sure that the leaves and trunk are well sprayed.

Remember

to keep turning the topsoil to facilitate the absorption of water, to let the roots breathe and prevent a harmful crust forming.

Protect your houseplants from draughts, even in the warmer weather. Leave the less delicate plants out in any gentle rain for one or two hours at a time. The rainwater will wash the leaves and the plant will take in plenty of fresh air.

Never use cold water for spraying or watering.

JUNE

A careful disinfectant programme

The summer is the happiest time of the year for houseplants and it should not produce any unpleasant surprises. The main problem arises because more frequent watering (which is necessary during the warmer months) also produces ideal conditions for germs and bacteria.

It is therefore advisable to intensify the disinfectant programme. The plants require more regular feeding and an occasional spraying with a foliar feed will be of benefit.

Protection from the sun's rays

The June sun is very strong and can cause considerable damage to the foliage, especially if it is wet.

Remember

to layer any plants which are propagated by this technique. The sap is at its most active at this time of year and new roots will form very rapidly.

Cut away any unwanted stems (just above one of the many tufts of aerial roots) of the scindapsus and philodendron if they are growing too long.

If you want to increase your stock, these cuttings can be put in a glass vase of water to form roots.

JULY

Be careful of the light
The same rules apply to July as to June. The only point to be particularly careful about, since July is often a very hot month, is to keep the rooms cool. But don't plunge your plants into semi-darkness by drawing the blinds! The best solution in a real heat-wave is to put all the houseplants together in one room and to keep this 'plant room' light, while the rest of the house can remain cool and shady.

Remember
to cover the topsoil with a layer of well moistened peat or moss if you are going away for the weekend. This will keep the earth cool and the plant healthy for four to five days.

Do *not* leave the windows of the 'plant room' open when you go out (even for a few hours). Storms blow up quickly without warning at this time of the year and a gust of wind could blow the plant pots over. Moreover, the temperature might suddenly drop several degrees which would seriously damage the plants.

Turn over the topsoil and give the plants a good watering. Spray the leaves, too, before going away on holiday.

AUGUST

Spraying is particularly important
During this very hot and sultry month the plants suffer from the lack of moisture in the atmosphere (and the lack of light if the curtains are kept closed). An occasional spray with tepid water will be appreciated on hot, dry days. Again, remember not to use cold water. Whenever possible, use rainwater when spraying and watering houseplants.

Remember
to protect the plants from direct sunlight, but give them plenty of diffused light.

Protect plants that are temporarily out on the balcony from heavy rain. Bring houseplants in at night if there is any sign of mist on the horizon.

Dose any plants that show signs of yellowing (usually a symptom of anaemia or chlorosis) with a chelated iron preparation.

SEPTEMBER

Give the plants less water
Houseplants need more or less the same treatment in September as they did in August but since the weather is probably considerably cooler during the second half of the month the plants may require less water.

Keep up the regular leaf spraying for the time being, but discontinue this at the end of the month to give the plants a chance to rest before winter sets in.

Winter bulbs
Winter flowering bulbs should be prepared towards the end of September. Hyacinth, tulip, crocus and narcissus bulbs can be planted at the end of September and forced to flower at Christmas time.

There are three different ways of doing this:
☐ Hyacinths can be grown in water.
☐ Tulips, narcissi or crocuses can be grown in peat or bulb fibre.
☐ Narcissi or crocuses can be grown in gravel.

Remember
to bring in the cacti which have spent the summer outside.

Close the windows in the evening if the temperature falls below 20°C (68°F) or if a storm is brewing. Protect houseplants from the rain since this will be too cold by now and could ruin the foliage.

OCTOBER

The return of the cold weather
The cold weather is back again. Do not open the windows near your houseplants since cold draughts could damage them.

Now is the time to re-pot plants which have been growing in the same container for more than a year, or which appear to need it. The soil will have lost most of its nutritive value by now so the plant should be transferred to a slightly larger pot to allow room for further growth.

Generally speaking, the new pot should be about 2 cm (1 in) larger in diameter than the previous one to allow room for the new roots which will form next spring.

Remember
to water the soil before taking the plant out of its old pot. If the roots do not come out easily it is preferable to break the pot rather than the roots.

If possible, use a compost which has been specially prepared for houseplants. This has numerous advantages: permeability, absorbency, etc.

Try growing some of your houseplants in water. This takes care of watering problems and ensures a regular and continuous feeding for the plants.

NOVEMBER

Keep the windows closed and give the plants less water
In October there may have been a few warm days when the windows were briefly opened, but the mists and fogs

The beautiful variegated leaves of the croton make this a very elegant and attractive houseplant.

and sudden unpredictable changes of temperature in November make it imperative to keep windows near houseplants firmly closed. Remember not to move the pots about too much. This wastes valuable energy.

Remember
to reduce watering. Every species has its own particular requirements but it is best to be on the stingy side when watering at this time of the year since excessive moisture could result in root rot.

Use a suitable leaf polish for cleaning the leaves. If you are using an aerosol spray, remember to stand at least 30 cm (12 in) away from the plant.

DECEMBER

A moderate temperature and frequent spraying
The 'difficult' season for houseplants is here again. They should be kept in a maximum temperature of 18–20°C (65–70°F), away from heat sources and draughts. They should not be moved because each change of position means that the plant must waste energy in reorientating itself correctly towards the light.

Keep the soil moist but not waterlogged. Spray the leaves occasionally to compensate for the hot atmosphere and lack of moisture in the air.

Remember
always to use water at room temperature for watering and spraying.

Check bulbs frequently to make sure that they are healthy.

HYDROPONICS

The various stages of transferring a scindapsus from an ordinary pot with soil into a special hydroponic vase. The necessary equipment for hydroponic cultivation: a glass vase, the special grid, a few stones and some nutrient pills (ordinary houseplant fertilizer will do just as well) (1). First of all, the plant must be taken out of its terracotta pot (2), then washed in tepid water (3) to remove all the soil from its roots (4 and 5). At this point, the roots can be passed through the holes in the grid (6) and the grid fixed in place in the vase (7). Finally, the grid is filled with stones to keep the plant upright (8).

Nearly all houseplants, even those normally requiring little water, can be successfully grown in water moreover, the pattern made by a plant's delicate roots becomes an additional fascinating feature.

To understand the enormous potential of this type of cultivation, two points should be borne in mind:

☐ In order to survive, plants absorb a number of organic and mineral substances which are dissolved in rain or other water (see section on 'Feeding', page 9).
☐ The soil serves to support the roots and to anchor the plant to its source of food.

So we can conclude that it is really the water and not the soil which is indispensable to the plant, provided that it contains the correct nutritive elements.

On the basis of this assumption, several experiments were carried out during World War II to find out if hydroponic techniques could be used to produce fresh vegetables out of season. From these first attempts, which were subsequently perfected in a Californian institute, we have now arrived at a hydroponic technique which can be used for houseplants.

This hydroponic technique is not to be confused with that under the registered name of 'Hydroculture', which makes use of special clay granules and a special long-term fertilizer in pur-nade pots.

Vases and nutrient pills
Suitable glass vases, which are available in sizes from 500 ml to 3 litres (1–5 pints), with a special grid to support the roots, are best for hydroponic cultivation.

The grid is concave so that it can hold a certain quantity of small stones which will help to hold the plant upright and stop the trunk slipping down into the water. There are 31 notches round the edge of the grid, one for each day of the month. There is a small movable metal tab which can be placed in one of the notches to indicate which day the water was changed and the nutrient pills given. One pill is sufficient for 1 litre (nearly 2 pints) of water and this will provide all the food the plant requires: phosphorous, potassium, nitrogen, magnesium, sulphur, calcium, zinc, iron, copper and manganese.

Which are the most suitable plants?

Nearly all houseplants, including succulents (even though these normally require very little water).

They quickly adapt to an aquatic life and absorb the correct moisture as and when they need it. Some species are more suitable than others: coleus, papyrus, dieffenbachia, dracaena, hedera, ferns, ficus, philodendron, peperomia, pilea, scindapsus, sansevieria, syngonium, spathiphyllum, tetrastigma, tradescantia. It is generally a good idea to use young plants as they adapt more quickly and with less difficulty than older ones.

This critical adaptation period lasts about a month, during which time the old roots drop off and new fleshy white 'aquatic' roots are formed. These new roots will absorb the nutritive substances in the water very rapidly as they are specially adapted for the purpose.

How and when to prepare the plants

Obviously you cannot just put any plant into a vase of water and expect it to grow successfully. For this technique to be successful, the following rules must be observed:

The most favourable season

Summer is the best time of year to start growing a plant in water as the sap is at its most active then and there is plenty of oxygen in the air. If this operation is carried out in January, the plant must be kept in a very light environment at a constant tempera-

5

6

7

8

ture of 18–20°C (65–70°F). If these conditions are not available it would be advisable to leave this task to a specialist.

The most suitable plants

As already mentioned, young plants are best suited to this technique.

How to uproot the plant

This should be carried out with extreme care. The plant must be removed from its pot without damaging the roots. Remember to water the soil thoroughly before starting work. If, in spite of this precaution, the plant still refuses to come out, it is preferable to break the pot with

a hammer rather than to risk damaging the roots.

Washing the roots

The tuft of roots must be washed gently with several changes of tepid water to remove all traces of soil.

Arranging the plant in its glass vase

The roots must be passed through the holes in the special grid in such a way as to keep the plant evenly balanced in the vase. The holes can then be filled with small stones and bog or sphagnum moss to fix the plant securely in position. If the plant is very tall and slender, or a climber, it will

need a plastic stake (there are two holes in the grid specially designed to hold stakes).

Pouring in the water

The water must be at room temperature, and there should be a gap for air at least 3 cm (1 in) deep between the base of the grid and the water; this air cushion is necessary to allow the roots room to breathe.

The rest period

During the first couple of weeks of its new life in water, the plant will pass through a period of adjustment during which time it will be losing its old roots and forming new aquatic ones. Do not add any

1. *Most houseplants can be grown in water, like these two: a dieffenbachia (the lower plant) and a scindapsus (the higher plant); even some succulent plants can be successfully grown in this way if they receive sufficient light because the roots will only absorb the amount of water they need.*
2. *This picture shows several species growing in water. From the left: caladium, dieffenbachia, aloe, dracaena, another caladium, spathiphyllum and philodendron (P. scandens). The hydroponic vases come in various sizes, from 500 ml (1 pint) to 5 litres (9 pints), and some can even be hung on the wall.*

2

nutrient pills to the water during this phase, because the plant must be given a chance to rest while it is becoming acclimatized to its new form of life. After approximately two weeks, when the old roots show signs of dropping off, new fleshy white roots will begin to form at the base of the plant and in no time at all, these will spread all over the vase.

Changing the water
The first change of water should be made 25–30 days after the plant was first put in water and subsequently at intervals of 25–30 days. Always use water at room temperature, containing the appropriate amount of nutrient (one pill is sufficient for 1 litre or nearly 2 pints of water). Just lift the grid with the plant on it, pour away the old water, add the fresh water and nutrient solution and put the grid back into position again.

Cleaning the leaves
It is advisable to keep the leaves scrupulously clean by spraying them once a week with a good combined leaf polish and disinfectant.

BOTTLE GARDENS

1

2

*The mass of beautiful
shapes and colours of an exotic tropical forest can
be contained within the glass wall
of a goldfish bowl.*

A bottle garden makes an extremely attractive indoor ornament. It is a kind of miniature greenhouse contained in a glass receptacle, often a goldfish bowl.

The bottle garden can be of any shape: a large glass bowl or chalice, a wide-mouthed flask, or the more traditional semi-sphere. Carboys and demijohns, or even a small fish tank about 40 cm long and 20 cm wide (16 in long and 8 in wide) also make excellent bottle gardens.

A constant temperature and humidity level
You may wonder what ad- vantages a bottle garden has over the more traditional methods. In a bottle garden the plants enjoy the same ideal conditions as they would in a greenhouse. The humidity level remains constant since any water vapour quickly condenses on the glass sides and falls down to earth as water droplets. This process repeats itself over and over again. For this reason, plants growing in a bottle garden do not need nearly as much water as those in ordinary pots. A spoonful of water every week will replace any moisture that has been lost through evaporation.

1–2. Houseplants can be grown in greenhouse conditions in a bottle garden. The leaves of the various plants look most attractive when seen through the glass walls of the container.

Besides making watering less of a chore, the bottle garden will keep the plants at a constant temperature, protected from the danger of draughts or sudden changes of temperature brought on by open doors or windows.

The constant high humidity level also helps the plants through the winter period when many houseplants suffer from dehydration in an overheated atmosphere.

How to make a bottle garden
A bottle garden is not difficult to prepare but it is important to work with care and to choose small, young plants. If older, more developed plants are used then the pleasure of watching them change and grow from day to day will be lost. The curved sides of the garden distort the leaves and plants to produce an undreamed of mass of beautiful shapes and colours.

3

4

3–7. *This shows how to prepare a bottle garden: first, find a suitable container and plants (3); put a layer of small stones and a layer of wood charcoal on the bottom (4), pour 6–7 cm (2–3 in) of compost mixed with peat and sand on top of this (5). Arrange the plants (6), taking care to cover the roots with compost and a layer of moss (7).*

This is what you do:

☐ On the bottom of the bottle place some small stones and then a layer of wood charcoal. This will prevent the roots from coming into contact with any water which may accumulate on the bottom.

☐ On top of this, arrange a 6–7 cm (2–3 in) layer of peat mixed with soil and sand. It is a good idea to use a cardboard funnel for this to prevent the glass sides of the garden from getting dirty.

☐ Arrange a few small plants and some interesting rocks, dry roots, fir cones, shells etc. on top of this soil mixture.

☐ Cover the plant roots with a little compost and a layer of moss.

Finally, add a little water and spray the leaves. Make sure the bottle garden has plenty of light, away from direct sunlight and heat sources.

5

6

7

8

9

10

8–9–10. *Some bottle gardens of various shapes and sizes. A sensible combination of plants and ease of watering make this an ideal way to* *grow even the most delicate houseplants. Succulent plants can often be brought into flower in a bottle garden.*

The most suitable species

Because of their humid hot-house atmosphere bottle gardens are suitable for all types of houseplant, especially those which need cool soil and a humid atmosphere.

These small plants are particularly suitable: asplenium, spathiphyllum, selaginella, scindapsus, ferns, some palms and tradescantia.

Of course, if the moisture level is kept low and the bottle garden is only watered once a month, even succulent plants will grow very happily in this way.

Four examples of the ancient Japanese art of bonsai. Only a few centimetres tall, these trees are between five and fifteen years old. 1 Cypress; 2 Maple; 3 Quince; 4 Yew.

*A landscaped garden of full-grown oak,
maple and pine trees
or an orchard of cherry, plum and
apple trees can be confined to
an earthenware bowl on a table top.*

A beautiful Chinese juniper.

These are miniature trees which, if growing naturally, would reach 10–20 m (30–60 ft) high, but by using the bonsai technique, they are grown in a bowl and do not reach more than 50–60 cm (20–25 in) even after many years.

A miracle? It would seem so. A miracle of patience and skill in which the Japanese have been acknowledged masters for thousands of years.

Those who have not seen a bonsai tree close to, would find it hard to understand the beauty of these trees growing only a few centimetres high in bowls where entire landscapes have been recreated in miniature, with rocks, moss and a few tiny dead leaves round the gnarled roots of the tree.

Is a bonsai tree difficult to keep?

It is not easy unless certain rules are carefully followed. It is impossible to give all the necessary rules in great detail as they vary so much from species to species. Here is a summary of the most basic rules:

☐ Bonsai trees must be kept in the open all the year round. In summer, during the heat of the day, the plants should be protected from the sun's rays. In winter they should be placed in the sunniest spot available.

☐ Bonsai trees need plenty of fresh air, but strong winds can be damaging, so they must be sheltered when necessary.

☐ Dust, soot, smoke and dryness are their worst enemies.

☐ Do not keep bonsai trees near railway lines or busy roads as the vibrations would be harmful.

☐ Bonsai trees do not like sudden changes of temperature: they therefore need to be sheltered during the night.

When and how much water

Watering is probably the most important and the most difficult aspect of looking after bonsai trees. It is impossible to make hard and fast rules as regards quantity and frequency as each plant varies in this respect.

However, here are a few basic guidelines:

☐ Water with great care so as not to expose the roots.

☐ Give the tree some water as soon as the soil looks dry because dehydration is very damaging.

1. *A red Japanese maple in full spring glory just as the first leaves appear. This is a very rare species.*
2. *A tiny apple tree about to flower. In spite of its size this tree produces perfect though small fruit every year like a normal apple tree.*

□ The water must always be at environmental temperature.

□ The soil should be evenly moist all over with no dry patches. Make sure the water has gone right through the soil.

□ In summer the plants need plenty of water (water twice a day if this appears necessary: in the morning and in the evening).

□ In the autumn the quantity of water should be reduced.

□ In winter, continue watering, but make sure the water does not freeze in the pot. It is advisable to water at midday when the air is at its warmest.

The different forms of bonsai tree

It is quite possible to find bonsai trees at reasonable prices in flower shops, in specialist nurseries or offered for sale in newspapers and magazines. Apart from the variety of species grown (pine, oak, maple, ilex, cherry, plum etc.) there are also many different forms of bonsai, some more or less contorted, which give the tree a special dramatic fascination.

Characteristic forms for bonsai trees

Chokkan (*straight trunk or upright*)
The only type with slender trunk.
Shakan (*oblique or very sloping trunk*)
Looks like a windswept tree near the sea or in the mountains.
Kengai (*bent trunk or cascading*)
The trunk leans right out of the bowl.
Hankan (*gnarled or almost spiral trunk*)
Looks like a tree distorted by years of bad weather.
Sokan (*double trunk*)
Two trunks growing from the same stump.

Kabudachi (*a group of trees*)
Several trunks growing from the same stump.
Netsuranari (*separate trunks growing from the same root*)
Several trunks.
Yoseue (*collective plant*)
Like a miniature wood.
Ishizuki (*tree with stone*)
The tree trunk grows round a rock.

IKEBANA

1

2

Ikebana is a special way of arranging flowers according to modern versions of precise rules laid down by an ancient tradition. It is not an easy art to master but there are several ikebana schools in Europe.
1. A few maranta leaves, a branch of cymbidium orchids and some curls of rattan cane form this 'Nageire' arrangement in a tall, narrow vase.
2. Roses and branches of mahonia make up this 'Moribana' arrangement in a low, wide bowl.
3. Another 'Moribana' arrangement with agapanthus, azalea leaves and bleached, dried genista.

3

This Japanese word (made up of 'ike' or 'living' and 'hana' or 'flower, leaf, blade of grass' or all that is green and beautiful) can be interpreted as 'living flowers'.

In the West the word 'ikebana' is used to describe the Japanese technique of arranging flowers, which is really an art form in itself. It is not necessary to use particularly expensive flowers for ikebana. Even roots, distorted branches, shells, stones and a variety of other objects can be incorporated in a composition provided they can be arranged in such a way as to describe a situation, a dance movement, an atmosphere or even a feeling.

A very ancient tradition
Today the art of ikebana is known and appreciated all over the world. In many countries there are schools which teach this difficult

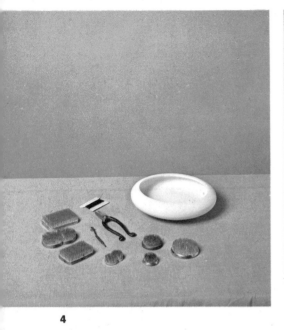

4

5

6

10

11

12

Here are the various stages in an ikebana arrangement.
4. *The material you need: a bowl, secateurs and pinholders.*
5. *First place the pinholder and some water in the container.*
6. *Cut the tallest stem to the correct length.*
7. *Bend the branch to give it a curve.*
8. *Arrange the tallest branch first as this defines the lines and proportions for the rest of the composition.*

method of arranging flowers and leaves according to precise rules, representing a ritualistic symbolism through the various elements in the composition, the way in which they are arranged and even the very lengths of the flower stems.

The rules and traditions of ikebana are very old and come from the first floral gifts presented to Buddha. From this time on a precise set of rules relating to these floral gifts was established and, in approximately 600 AD, the first school of ikebana was founded in Kyoto.

Ever since that time, the symbolism of the 'living flower' has undergone a continual transformation so that today there are at least fourteen different styles of ikebana and many different schools of thought, both aesthetic and religious. In Japan alone there are several hundreds of these schools.

There are endless books on ikebana which describe in greater or lesser detail the principal rules of composition which must be learned before embarking on the first attempts at a 'Nageire' arrangement in its tall narrow

vase, or on a 'Moribana' in its low, wide bowl.

An essential material
Besides the flowers, leaves, branches, roots and the characteristic oriental vases with their precise lines and deep, cold colours, there is one other material you will need: a heavy metal support of pins (a 'pinholder') to hold the flowers and other items in place. Forked sticks to keep the stems apart at the neck of the vase and wire netting to put in high, narrow vases to hold the flowers in place are also useful. Once you have

7

8

9

13

14

15

gathered together all the necessary materials, it is essential to settle down to your ikebana arrangement with a certain degree of unhurried concentration and with a very precise mental picture of the arrangement you are attempting to create.

As a general rule, the easiest compositions are the ones which are triangular in shape with these three elements at the apex of the stems: heaven at the uppermost point, man in the middle and the earth at the lowest point.

How to preserve the flowers

Cut flowers will not have a very long life in the house, particularly in 'Moribana' arrangements where the flowers are arranged in a shallow, wide bowl, not more than 2–3 cm (1 in) deep, unless they are specially treated. Otherwise, your ikebana arrangement, which has taken so much hard work, will only last for a day or so and this would be a terrible waste.

The Japanese women, who are experts in this field, succeed in keeping their flowers in perfect condition for days

on end by frequent spraying, changes of water, sometimes several times a day and by protecting the flowers from draughts and changes of temperature. In Japan this last precaution is not too difficult since flower arrangements are often kept in a 'tokonoma', or niche containing a statue of Buddha dedicated to ancestors.

Ikebana is undoubtedly a valid and imaginative way of using flowers to create graceful compositions of unusual beauty, but it is a very difficult art to master.

9. *Once the principal branch has been arranged, fix the second branch in position.*
10. *Cut the flower stems on the slant while keeping them immersed in water.*
11–12–13. *Arrange the other elements in position.*
14. *The composition is complete apart from the finishing touches: cut away superfluous leaves and twigs.*
15. *Spray the entire arrangement to help preserve it for as long as possible.*

FLOWER ARRANGING

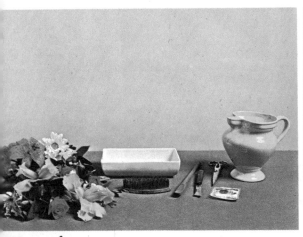

1

2

3

4

5

6

7

If you want to produce a pretty flower arrangement you must be methodical about it:
1. First prepare the necessary materials: flowers, container, jug of water, stem holder, scissors, small sharp knife or secateurs, special powder to prolong the life of the flowers and a spoon.
2. Put the flower holder in position.
3-4-5. Cut the flowers to length and begin the arrangement by fixing the longest and shortest flowers in place.
6. Fill in the gaps to produce the desired effect.

A wise oriental proverb says 'a woman is really beautiful if she knows how to make the best of what Nature gave her'.

The same can be said of flowers: their beauty is at its best when it is framed in the right setting. This basic rule applies equally to plants grown in the garden or on a balcony, but it is at its most valid in the case of cut flower arrangements to decorate the house.

Here are a few basic rules and practical suggestions for making an ordinary bunch of flowers into a beautiful arrangement.

How to choose the flowers
It is true to say that any type of flower can be used to good effect in an arrangement, but the following points should be remembered:
☐ If the flowers are picked from the garden they should be gathered in the morning while the day is still cool.
☐ They should be cut with proper secateurs. Use long-handled cutters for roses to avoid the thorns.
☐ When buying or picking flowers, choose ones that are not yet fully out but not too closed. Ideally, the buds should be sufficiently open to show the colour of the petals.
☐ When you get home, put the flowers in tepid water at once and make sure the entire stem is immersed. After two or three hours, you can proceed with your floral creation.
☐ During this 'rest' the bowl or bucket of flowers should be left in a cool, dark room.

How to prepare your arrangement
First of all, cut the stems to the desired length. It is advisable to cut the stems on a slant and make a nice clean cut so that the flowers will be able to absorb water more easily and will thus last longer. The cut is made on the slant to increase the surface area of cut tissue.

When this has been done, proceed as follows:
☐ Remove the leaves on the lower part of the stem as they

would tend to rot and turn the water foul.

☐ Never use cold water except for hollow-stemmed subjects such as narcissi. For roses and other woody-stemmed flowers it should be fairly hot.

☐ To prolong the life of your cut flowers it is a good idea to add a special powder to the water (available from flower shops). This powder prevents the formation of bacteria in the water and helps to keep the flowers alive for a reasonable length of time.

☐ A little fresh water should be added to the vase night and morning to replace any that has evaporated.

The type of vase

The vase should be well proportioned in relation to the height of the flowers and in a suitable style for the type of arrangement you wish to make. Here are a few helpful suggestions:

☐ Tall narrow vases: for flowers with long, leafless, rigid stems.

☐ Goblets: for elaborate fan shaped arrangements.

☐ Wide shallow bowls: suitable for ikebana compositions, or a low arrangement for the centre of the dining table.

☐ Jugs or vases with a handle, or asymmetrical vases: for arrangements that are higher on one side than the other.

☐ Vases of an unusual shape (a shell, a hollowed out stone, a money box, weighing scales, etc.): for unusual flowers, distorted branches, etc.

The rules relating to colour

When choosing a vase it is very important to pick the right colour in relation to the flowers, trying to achieve a pleasant contrast or harmonious combination of colours.

There is a precise parabola relating to colour combinations: purple—bright red—geranium red—orange—yellow—pale green—bright green — dark green — dark violet — bright violet — mauve — lilac — periwinkle

7–8. *Pour the special powder into the water and stir well with the spoon.*
9. *Fill the vase with water.*

8

9

10. *Admire your completed handiwork.*

10

blue — deep blue — dark blue —navy. White can be inserted between any two colours.

Flowers arranged according to this scheme can only produce a perfect chromatic result. The vase can be the same colour as one of the flowers, or white, or in copper, wood, brass, silver or bamboo. The arrangement can also consist of various shades, tints and tones of the same colour in a very sophisticated and complicated style.

If you want to make an arrangement using one dominant colour in various paler tints and darker shades, it is important not to use many leaves as too much greenery could detract from the delicate colouring of the flowers.

The style

We have discussed the best vases and colour combinations to use, but what about style? There are many different ways of arranging flowers to create certain lines. Here are a few:

Stylized
An arrangement made up of a few flowers together with other rather rigid elements: branches, large leaves, a candle, etc.
Ikebana
Very like the stylized arrangement, but following

You may combine fruits and vegetables, grasses and branches or stones and shells with flowers to good effect.

precise rules based on an oriental philosophy.

Mixed

Made up of all kinds of flowers in apparent disorder, based on a precise chromatic scheme and the size of the flower heads.

Symmetrical

Fan-shaped, semi-spherical, spherical, cone-shaped etc. These arrangements are also called 'formal' or 'classical'.

Asymmetrical

When the arrangement is deliberately uneven on one side

The pictures on these pages show various styles of flower arrangements: a stylized composition using anthurium flowers and leaves (1): an ikebana arrangement with orchids, fern fronds and dried seed pods (2); a modern asymmetrical style with lilies, begonia leaves, ferns and calathea (3); a classical asymmetrical style with lilies, gerbera, a rose, begonia leaves and ferns (4); an arrangement of flowers and fruit (5) opposite.

1

3

2

4

5

7

6

6. *Symmetrical arrangement of marguerites, freesias and heather*
7. *19th century style arrangement of lilies, alstroemeria, roses, lilac, gladioli, gerbera and heather.*

of the vase, usually but not necessarily to compensate for the asymmetry of the container.

How to arrange your flowers

Having selected your vase and prepared the flowers, now is the moment to 'create' your arrangement. These are the most important steps:

☐ Place a suitable flower holder at the bottom of the vase (there is a great variety of shapes and sizes of cushion or pinpoint flower holders with metal bristles on which the stalks can be inserted), or alternatively place a ball of large-mesh wire netting in the neck of the vase. These will hold the stems in position when changing the water, etc.

☐ Arrange the flowers, starting with the tallest and then filling in the gaps until the desired shape is created.

Finally, arrange the leaves in position to pull the whole composition together. They can also be used to fill in any unwanted gaps between the flowers which might otherwise make the arrangement look untidy.

☐ Pour water into the vase (remember to add the special powder to prolong the life of the flowers). If you are using a very wide shallow bowl or a particularly large bowl, it is advisable not to fill it with water until it is in position, taking great care not to spill any on the furniture or the floor.

A few helpful suggestions

Here are a few useful suggestions for arranging flowers:

☐ Little flowers are very useful for small arrangements.
☐ Large flowers are suitable for 'important' arrangements.

If they are to be used in small vases, they must be

117

very limited in number and should be arranged in a stylized or asymmetrical fashion, juxtaposed with slender, shorter flowers, preferably with distorted branches.

☐ Flowers for the dining table should be arranged in a low, compact composition, not more than 15–20 cm (6–8 in) high. They can be put in the centre of the table, at each end or in several individual bunches round the table.

☐ Flower arrangements for a formal dinner party, cold buffet or bar are most effective if they combine flowers with fruit and foliage. A table centre-piece of well chosen fruit, vegetables and foliage combining several colours can be very attractive: aubergines with carrots and lemons; black and white grapes with white and red radishes; oranges and mandarins with yellow onions and sprigs of cauliflower: tomatoes with cherries and peas; parsley, apricots and courgettes.

☐ Do not forget dried grasses, fruits, branches, fir cones, stones, shells, autumn leaves, seed pods, dried flowers, teasels and so on. These should be collected in the summer and autumn and they can provide the basis for any type of floral arrangement with flowers, foliage or fruit. Similarly, it is a good idea to collect any objects you come across which would be suitable for use as a vase or a support in a flower arrangement, even simple things like jam jars etc. These can easily be hidden behind a few leaves, two or three stones, a shell or a group of fir cones.

1. *Fruit, vegetables, freesias, iris and a frond of maidenhair fern in a pictorial arrangement.*
2. *This table centrepiece of dried flowers and two yellow candles would be very suitable for a formal dinner party. The candles are for decoration only.*
3. *A triangular arrangement of enchanting lilies, cornflowers and gladioli in a large shell.*

CUT FLOWERS

Graceful flowers deserve a better fate than to be jammed into a vase full of water. Here are some useful tips on how to make cut flowers last longer.

Growing garden flowers for use in the house is a very satisfying occupation for those who have a garden or balcony. Two or three window boxes can be reserved for flowers for use in the house. There are numerous species of plants which are easy to grow and flower profusely over a long period of time. But a successful arrangement of cut flowers does not depend solely on the efficient growing of the flowers. It is most important to learn how to maximize the length of life of the flowers once they have been brought into the house.

The following simple rules also apply to cut flowers bought from a flower shop, market or street stall, which all too often begin to wilt after only a few hours. This is sometimes because they were not freshly cut, but more often because people do not know how to treat cut flowers in order to keep them alive as long as possible.

Two important operations
We shall begin by defining two operations which must be carried out if the cut flowers are to survive for any length of time:
□ The flower stems absorb water through cells along their entire length. If the cells at the cut end of the stalk are crushed, or begin to rot, the water cannot penetrate the tissues and conse-quently the flower head does not receive the moisture it needs. This is why it is so important to make a clean cut, preferably with a sharp knife.
□ The life span of cut flowers depends to a very large extent on the 'quality' of the water. Flowers need plenty of oxygen. This will enable them to 'breathe' properly which will help them to keep their beauty for several days.
□ A nutrient made specially for cut flowers, e.g. crysal, helps to prolong their life and prevents the water from turning foul. It is not neces-sary to change the water with this method and the flowers will stay fresh for at least two or three times as long as usual.

The choice of vase
Even the choice of vase is im-portant. Quite apart from any aesthetic consideration (shape, colour etc.) it is very important to remember that cut flowers need a great deal of water, space and light. They must be able to drink plenty of water and should not be squeezed into a tight

Preparing an attractive arrangement of cut flowers is skilled work, but with patience and application excellent results can be produced, provided that fresh flowers are used. For this reason, it is important to pick the flowers at the right moment and know how to treat them to keep them alive as long as possible.

necked vase. They should be kept in a well lit position away from direct sunlight. All the leaves must be re-moved from the portion of the stem which will be immersed in water: any leaves acci-dently left on this portion of the stalk would absorb water to no good purpose and would greatly increase the con-sumption of oxygen, which could lead to rot.

One rule for each species
So far we have only dis-cussed general rules but we should point out that not all flowers require the same treatment. This will depend on the different structure of the flower stems. These can be hollow, woody, of a very succulent consistency, exude sap, etc. These species all require different treatment as soon as they have been picked or brought home.

Put all cut flowers in a bucket of water, immersing the stems (having removed all the lower leaves) right up to the flower head. The flowers should be left to rest in the bucket for at least two or three hours, preferably overnight, in a cool, dark place. When you have a suit-able vase, proceed as follows:

Woody stems
The lower portion (5–6 cm or 2 in) of the stalk should be stripped of its bark and the end should be split upwards for about 3 cm (1 in) with a sharp knife. This treatment is particularly applicable to flowering shrubs and herba-ceous perennials with very thick stems.

Hollow stems or stems which exude sap
These should be 'cauterized', or held over a gas or candle flame for several seconds. It is a good idea to protect the flower heads with a piece of

paper when you are doing this. When the stems have been cauterized (the lower 5–6 cm or 2 in) pour plenty of cold water over them and leave them in a bucket of water for at least an hour before proceeding with the arrangement.

Stems with thick, spongy pith

These require special treatment. Wrap the flowers in paper, then stand the ends of the stems in a few centimetres of boiling water for two or three minutes. Put the flowers in a vase of cold water.

Can faded flowers be revived?

If, in spite of all the correct treatment, your bunch of flowers begins to wilt and the flower heads droop as if the stalks were too exhausted to hold them up any longer, you can attempt (often with successful results) to revive their lost vigour and beauty by giving them a hot foot-bath. Even if it seems utterly crazy to treat a bunch of wilting roses, for example, in this way proceed as follows and they may regain their lost beauty:

☐ Fill a vase with 10 cm (4 in) of boiling water and put the roses in it. When the water has cooled down and is tepid to the touch, fill the vase right up with tepid water. In the space of an hour the roses should have completely recovered their former looks.

☐ The same result can be achieved by lying the roses in a basin of tepid water (not boiling) and leaving them there until the water is cold. Just cut off the lower ends of the stems and your flowers will be as good as new. This often works wonders with all woody flowers.

Flower picking

We have briefly discussed ways of prolonging the life of cut flowers but we must not forget the actual picking operation itself, which should be carried out according to certain rules. Flowers must always be picked early in the morning, in dry and still weather.

Choose flowers that are just coming out, not too closed nor too open. Dahlias are an exception to this rule since they should be fully out when picked, otherwise the buds will wilt and drop off.

1–2–3. Three vases of cut flowers: gerbera with maranta leaves (1); agapanthus and African marigolds (2); lilies, fern fronds and oak leaves (3). There is a special powder which can be added to the water to prolong the life of cut flowers.

INDEX

125